Eldred J  3 in Egypt where his Health for Cairo. The 1936 and Eldred att school in Exmouth, Devon, whence he won an exhibition to Blundells in Tiverton and thence a State Scholorship to University College Hospital, London, qualifying in 1956.

Hospital appointments were followed by thee years' National Service in the Royal Navy and then a General Practice traineeship. While in the Navy he met and married Joy in Plymouth and in 1961 they emigrated to her home country, New Zealand, where he ran his private practice until retiring in 1998 to England.

They have two daughters, two sons and three grandchildren (so far!). He and Joy live in "a wee thatched matchbox" surrounded by fields of barley and sugar beet in Norfolk. He paints in oils and watercolour but their main hobby is gardening and criticising all sport on TV. In his retirement Eldred has been an enthusiastic volunteer worker in hospices in New Zealand and the UK.

Published by

MELROSE BOOKS

An Imprint of Melrose Press Limited
St Thomas Place, Ely
Cambridgeshire
CB7 4GG, UK
www.melrosebooks.com

FIRST EDITION

Copyright © Eldred Williams 2006

The Author asserts his moral right to
be identified as the author of this work

ISBN 1 905226 73 X

and bound in Great Britain by:
y Rowe, Bumpers Farm,
, Wiltshire, SN14 6LH, UK

"*NEVER MIND*".

Eldred Williams

Dedication

This little book is dedicated to my dearest, that is my wife Joy and our children Amanda, Susan, Timothy and Simon and my sister Diana.

Acknowledgement

The articles in this book have been reproduced with the kind permission of CMPMedica NZ Ltd.

Contents

Introduction

My family gave me a bicycle for my sixty-ninth birthday, and on calm, windless, dry days I take great delight in pedalling around the almost traffic-free back lanes of rural Norfolk, admiring the countryside and breathing the pure air.

I was doing just such one winter morning; there were rooks on the plough, a pheasant in the grass verge, fieldfares cackling overhead, pigeons attacking ivy berries in the hedgerows, a lonely column of thin brown smoke rising from a farmhouse chimney, and a vista of rolling (no, Norfolk is NOT flat) winter wheat and barley fields, interspersed with little woods and spinneys. I wax lyrical. It was so beautiful, so tranquil and I was so relaxed that I fell off my bike … It went into one ditch and I rolled across the lane into the other. (Had this been the A11 I would have been squashed flat the moment I hit the road). I remounted. And then I began to laugh. Imagine the scene. This stupid old crone, slowly pedalling away to nowhere. Paying no attention, bike and rider tilt over, further and further

... and further, so far that he falls off. Gets up, adjusts dress, retrieves bike, and rides slowly on, and (I bet you hadn't thought of this), laughing out loud like a hyena, in space, nowhere, to no one. And the more I laughed at the spectacle (go back two sentences, please) the more I laughed. It was a vicious circle. This old crone ... pedalling ... falling ... laughing ... This time I dismounted in an orderly fashion, but trembling with mirth, drew hanky to mop streaming cheeks of merriment, and peer apologetically at the disapproving pheasant. The rooks ignored me.

Explanation

This is a collection of very short stories which you can leave on the coffee table, or in the waiting room or, depending on your personal habits, might help to while away the time during the daily sojourn in the smallest room in the house.

They are not in chronological or any particular order for this is not an autobiography. Only one is pure fiction, all the others are, for the most part, painfully true.

I wrote them when the events were fresh in my mind, most over a period of about four years, at the request of the New Zealand Journal of General Practice, which published them at roughly monthly intervals. The majority have a medical flavour because I am a doctor, but there is little technical jargon so that the lay reader will have no difficulty in following the thrust of my prose. I have tested it on a friend of mine who could not be described as an intellectual force, and he laughed heartily at each story including the two poignant ones, so you see what I mean.

There is also a powerful New Zealand slant because I spent nearly all my working life there, but there are almost no instances where I felt it necessary to append explanatory notes for the United Kingdom populace. English is the native tongue, even for the Maoris, although the British Home Office do not believe this because when my wife, a Kiwi, applied in this year of 2005 for British citizenship, the H.O. insisted she obtain a certificate from a notary public to confirm that she could understand AND SPEAK her own, and, ipso facto, our, native tongue. This cost an extra £90 on top of the £214 application fee. In due course, at the swearing in ceremony, she was presented with a pretend vellum stating she was now one of us, and, rather quaintly, a green plastic biro pen stamped "Norfolk County Council".

But I digress. New Zealand is very like Britain except that it is quite different. You don't hoover, you lux; curtains are drapes; you are crook, not ill; you don't go shopping, you get the messages, showing, I understand, a mix of American, Australian and Scottish origins. There are many others, but the patients are the same as here. Testing a little old lady's hearing, I stood behind her and said, 'Can you hear me now?' to which she replied, 'No, Doctor'.

In these pages I laugh at a lot of people. I hope the reader will forgive me. Most of them are me.

NEVER MIND.

I'll Never Forget What's-his-Name

Dealing with people as we do, it is absolutely essential for GPs to be good with names. I am not. I never have been, and it would have been immeasurably more satisfactory if I had been an engineer or something.

But I am not, and I have had to carry this cross as best I may, and so have my patients, some of whom have become accustomed over the years to being called nothing, or 'Er', or a curious mixture of their own names. I think it must be my own private form of dyslexia which leads me to give vent to such mental mix-ups as calling a Mr Frederick Williams 'Bill', and Trevor Francis 'Frank'.

Mind you, I have worked on it; I do try. The results are ludicrous. One method is to try an association of ideas. Mrs Ann Sparrow ... well that's easy, think of a bird and then, go on, I introduce her as Tessa Finch. Likewise, an eminent colleague rejoices in a first name of Tudor, and when I introduce another eminent colleague to him I am conscious that the royal family will give me the clue and, wait for it, 'I'd like you to meet Windsor ...'

I have even forgotten my wife's name before now, which has led to a certain scepticism among the audience, rotten lot, but it makes it much worse if you make up a name on the spur of the moment.

Raised Eyebrows

And then again, there is the matter of seeing people out of bed. I mean, GPs, perforce, see people in bed more than anyone else, and they do look quite different when dressed and standing up. Before now I have raised eyebrows at social occasions by unthinkingly explaining that I didn't recognise so-and-so's wife out of bed, or, ipso facto, with clothes on.

I seldom forget a face but I rarely know who they are. I can recall their ailment or their gall-bladder with ease, and I have become pretty adept at verbal fencing until I have accumulated enough information to know who they are, although I won't get their names if I try until hell freezes over.

Television has made life miserable for me. Until TV was invented, most of the humans I knew were patients, and the remainder family and friends. Now the whole world has entered my circle and increased my identification problems a trillionfold.

A Familiar Face

A couple of years ago I was in England, visiting old friends in Southampton. As I got off the train I bumped into a very familiar face. I smiled and, because I didn't really expect to see anyone I knew so far from home except my old friends, I said, 'Hallo there, I didn't expect to see you so far from home,' and he said, 'Well I live here now.' 'Goodness,' I said and then, 'Sorry, I'll have to buzz, I am meeting some old friends and there they are.' With this I left my buddy and hastened over to where they stood.

We exchanged greetings and when the chatter died down a bit later I told them of the amazing coincidence of meeting a chap that I knew on the platform all this way from New Zealand, but I couldn't remember his name. 'Well, that was David Frost you patted on the shoulder,' they replied. 'He's lived in Southampton for years as far as we know.'

The Lackey at Kaiteriteri

Then there was the lackey who could be seen each day at Kaiteriteri helping the infirm and elderly and me and other poor balancers up the plank onto the water taxi from the beach for a day's sightseeing, a year or two ago.

He was a pleasant old chap, perhaps not that old but wearing a bit. Very civil, anyhow, clearly retired and probably picking up a few cents for helping the boatmen while staying with relatives in the camp; what a lucky old fellow, instead of the usual sweat and grind of the rest home or the state cottage with meals on wheels Monday to Friday and the home help two hours a week to do the luxing and ironing.

What was more surprising to me was that I knew that I knew him. His face was very familiar but so was that measured, almost educated speech. Had he been one of my hemiplegias, and recovered very well indeed? It didn't ring a bell. Perhaps a coronary or two, but that must have been quite a while ago.

I tried to imagine him in the far south where I live,

the cold wind tearing at his jacket, the snow on the hills, a miserable gas fire in the bedroom only furnished with a wooden chair, lino on the floor.

'Doc, it's the screws in my joints,' I tried to hear him saying, but I couldn't. Well a prostate then, that must be it, he looks so different in shorts and bare feet on the beach holding the boat steady as the sea surged around his surprisingly muscular and brown legs. His eye was steely but twinkled and his grip was firm. I certainly must have made a very good job of him, whatever it was he had had.

Incognito

My wife hates boats and never goes on trips on them with me, so I was telling her about this chap, still trying to place him in my mind. I had actually talked to him quite a bit on the return trip, trying to get clues to work on, but I was defeated.

My wife is fairly familiar with my deficit in the field of recognition. She listened to me with dancing eyes and a little dimple in the cheek which, experience told me, meant that I was in for the big one. 'Yes,' she said, 'Shirley was telling me about the spare hand Ralph has on the boat for a fortnight. He does it for fun, a bit incognito. He's called Beattie. I believe he's the Governor General of New Zealand.'

The Dawlish Warren Debacle

I don't look forward to things anymore. I mean pleasurable things. I get none of the fun of anticipation – if they turned out well, I only reap the pleasure of reflecting about them afterwards.

My family say I'm a cynic, that I am negative. The former may be correct, but I dispute the latter. That word has become one of the 'in' words of recent times, like the phrase 'out there' – everything is going on 'out there' these days, just as not long ago everything was 'at this point in time'. Before that it was 'this is right', a phrase which became so beloved by one patient of mine that it became impossible to obtain a history because even my 'Good morning, how are you?' opening was responded to with 'This is right', as was every other question, and the conversation became a farce. (Which is what it so often is anyhow … see … a cynic.)

Blameless Years

No, not negative, but a pessimist, yes, and a misanthrope

to boot. My family, if severely honest, will concede that I was not born this way. Up until a projected trip to Dawlish Warren, I had enjoyed six blameless years of fun and frolics, including the pleasurable anticipation of same. That is, with the exception of my second day at school. When I was taken to school on the first day, I was mollified at the knowledge of losing a day playing on the beach by the prospect of something new, something possibly titillating, a fresh avenue. Well, it turned out that it wasn't a bad day; it was new, but it was not all that interesting, and there was yet much to be done on the beach. So it was with mortification and not a little resentment that I learned that I was expected to go back not only for another day at the institution, but for dozens if not possibly hundreds more days, in fact someone seemed to have mortgaged my life (which in fact was the case).

But I digress.

At that age my psyche was sufficiently elastic to absorb the true horror of it all, but when I reached the age of six I had matured sufficiently to know the world. I knew the good from the bad, and I knew when a bull market would not yield me a bear. If, perchance, it did, then I would be warped forever, a misanthropic pessimist, positively pessimistic, not negative. Well it did, I got a five when I knew the card was an ace, and I've been like it ever since, even after the Dawlish Warren debacle.

A Thoroughly Romantic Spot

For those of you with a limited knowledge of the south coast of Devonshire in England, Dawlish Warren is a spit of sand at the mouth of the River Exe, with a few acres of marram grass, sea pinks and driftwood on it – actually an island during all but the lowest tides, and a most exciting and thoroughly romantic spot for the under ten age group. This was especially so because access was by sea, viz an elderly boatman who quoted a lower estimate than his older cobber to row the family across the twenty yards of placid water in his little wooden boat. He then left you, think of it, literally *marooned* on this desert island for two hours of wild adventure a la R Crusoe or the Swiss Family (why were all these people called Robinson, does anyone know?) and a picnic tea, before returning to collect you and his half crown from Father at 5 p.m.

A treat of a lifetime, and one which I had happily experienced twice so far, and for my sixth birthday the parents announced that this Valhalla of delight for a small boy was to be the order of the day, accompanied by one of or two very special, very privileged chums. How far ahead was The Day? I counted the days off one by one. They crawled by. We plotted all sorts of plans to hid in the marram grass away from the grown-ups, all manner of hunting of the wild animals imagined to be there; we would all be Mr Crusoe because no one wanted to be Man Friday; we would catch sharks in the (two inch high) surf. Golly only one more day to wait, and then it was The Day.

And it was off! Off? Off. Cancelled. Not on. Struck. Off. We weren't going. We couldn't go. 'Perhaps one day.'

The Reason

Even at age three I knew what that phrase meant, and I was right. Fifty years later and we still haven't been. And the reason? Well, you won't guess it in another fifty years of trying. No, I hadn't set fire to the hens, nor had I pinched the neighbours' plums again. I ate all my tapioca (if with some retching), and I had written a thank you letter to my uncle for the lousy model boat he'd sent me the previous Christmas, so crude in its construction that a baby would have scorned it.

Then again, the elderly boatman and his older cobber had not died, nor had they lost their boats. The Warren was still there, unaffected by storms, and we still lived within a mile of the beach opposite. I had not broken my leg, no one in the family had broken legs; the weather was perfect; school was over for the hols; what then could possibly abort the expedition?

Before I tell you, let me refer you to 9th November 1965. On that day, at a remote spot in the North American countryside, an overload switch in a junction box was subjected to a transient surge of power and it tripped, automatically rerouting the power to four other lines which, at that critical moment, were not ready for it, and they tripped. And most of the north-eastern United States was without power for a period ranging from hours to days. Airports went black as planes were about to land, traffic lights went out, all lights went out, trains stopped, machinery stopped, some people died, and, as a result of the enforced proximity of mixed couples in paralysed lifts, some people were born nine months later.

Mind-Blowing Result

You may know all this already, but I mention it because what you don't know until I tell you is that it was the second time in history that some apparently trivial, insignificant event resulted in mind-blowing disaster very many miles away. The first time in history was the disaster of not being able to go to Dawlish Warren on my birthday, and not even the most wise man of the east or anywhere would have put outside money on the reason for our trip being off being the crossing of the Polish frontier by German troops.

Who would have dreamed in their wildest moments that Hitler would ruin my day? Why me? Couldn't he see that war would be declared and all the beaches in the south of England closed with barbed wire against the expected invasion? How callous could the man get? By the time it was all over I was a teenager, not R Crusoe anymore, and anyway, we didn't live there by then.

So I never looked forward to anything anymore.

There is one PS to this, again Hitler's fault (he really had it in for me). After the Battle of the River Plate, the triumphant and shell-damaged HMS Exeter returned to her home port, and anchored at the mouth of the Exe, just off Dawlish Warren, for a hero's welcome. The whole population booked rides in boats to go out and board the ship and marvel at her wounds and mingle with her gallant crew. We booked our boat, and on the day a brisk wind got up, as did a choppy sea, and ours was the only boatman who declined to leave the safety of the harbour.

I decided to stay in bed for the rest of my life but in the end my parents talked me out of it. Next day, actually.

The Horns of a Dilemma

I must say that I have the greatest sympathy and, indeed, respect for murderers of the sort you read about in detective stories of the more old fashioned sort. I don't know if you have ever tried to dispose of a body but if you have not, take it from me, it's hard work.

I speak from a wealth of experience. Being endowed with a fairly large garden, I always bury mine. Dismembering is messy and incineration smelly, and I've never got around to more esoteric things like acid baths. I dig holes and in go the failures, to be removed from the sight of prying eyes for all time ... but this is where my regard for Agatha Christie's villains comes in.

Even on a cool day, with the earth softened by a week's rain, a six foot by two, and even only three feet deep, is hard and long work; in dry weather it is an ordeal of exertion, and once the corpse is in you've then got to fill it all in, and, of course, it never all goes back. You get left with a prodigious mound of earth and nowhere to put it. Then people come along and say 'What's that heap of earth, Doc? Been burying your failures, have you? Ha Ha Ha.' I could reply that I am making a new flower bed but it would hardly convince, out there in the paddock, and I usually laugh at their joke and tacitly agree.

But what gets me about the fictional murderers is that they do their interments in the dead of night, without a torch, and often do use a flower bed, having to dig up all the roses or petunias first (this still in the dark, and preferably soundlessly) having already covertly conveyed their victim to the spot. Being a small chap, I find I cannot carry bodies, I have to drag them, which would disqualify me right away. They dig their big deep hole, insert the contents, fill it up, and then replant all the flowers or parsnips exactly as they were before so that it takes the most efficient sleuth to crack the case. When I think how I puff and snort, grunt and groan, take hours and hours and then leave an untidy heap to boot, all overtly in broad daylight, I take my hat off to these professionals. They deserve to get away with it. I expect those who get a life sentence are much sought after as prison gardeners.

The other problem that I have not seen alluded to in the literature is that of spontaneous disinterment, or, quite simply, explosion. Again, I can draw from personal experience to advise my reader(s) that this is a hazard, and the fault, when it occurs, is mine for not digging the hole deep enough. I know six feet is the fashion in municipal graveyards, and perhaps this is what Ngaio Marsh's characters dig to, once they have the rhododendron bush out by the roots, but I baulk when I reach three feet, and in a stony patch or sun-baked or frozen soil I have had to settle for eighteen inches on occasions. Unless you have railway sleepers or ingots of pig iron to lend weight to the inadequate covering that results, you are treated to a spectacular if unwelcome reversal of all your efforts in a day or two, depending on the climate. Like a young volcano, the abdominal gases erupt forth, upwards and outwards, bearing on their evil exodus fragments of greenish skin, gut and sometimes bits of liver which whizz around like shrapnel, mindless of anyone in their path. The noise is quite impressive, too. Then one has to start all over again.

So the motto should always be to dig deep. I knew that when I buried Jocelyn, and yet I was too shallow, and the very top of her head protruded above the surface and was visible for many months afterwards; never a very pretty sight in life, this was not what we wanted all our guests to see, nor even the children, who might have had nightmares.

It reminds me of a story about Jocelyn which I still laugh about. One day (this was some time before she died) I was playing host to our local diabetes specialist after he had done a domiciliary visit with me (takes us back about ninety years, eh?). We were relaxing in the drawing room over a bottle of his favourite and mine, Tio Pepe, he facing the bay windows with the lawn beyond, me with my back to the same. I suppose we had had a glass or three and were chatting of this and that when suddenly his face froze, eyes staring and jaw slack; but in a trice he had composed himself and we carried on, I too polite to ask if he had fits of which I was unaware. Then it happened again, and this time he was not inclined to compose. He looked at his glass, put it down, and muttered something about DTs. 'I thought I saw something,' he said in reply to my concerned look. I turned and looked out of the window. Green sward and birds twittering; the occasional butterfly.

'Just the countryside,' I said cheerily. 'The trouble with you chaps is you spend all your lives in hospitals in the city. Let me refill your glass; I promise this is only sherry.' But I was only halfway through topping him up when it happened yet again. 'There,' he cried in a tremulous voice. 'Oh dear Lord, what in heaven's name is that awful spectacle?'

This time I saw her. Jocelyn, walking across the lawn. As I said before, even in life she was not a pretty sight. Try and imagine a very elderly goat with hindquarters shrivelled and atrophied by some progressive myelitis which had defeated the vet some years before so that really she was only half a goat who had developed the grotesque art of balancing and walking on her two front legs only, the weight of her enormous horns counterbalancing the withered posterior half so that she resembled an emu with hooved feet and shaggy mohair coat, wearing a Viking helmet from a stage show. Not, one has to admit, one's ordinary run of the mill nanny (and I suspect from her horns that she was a he anyhow). It took several more Tio Pepes to reassure Jack.

And then, as I was telling you, when Jocelyn reached the end of her days, I failed to take account of her horns in my digging, with the result that they stuck out above ground as a rather peculiar sort of self headstone until the ants had thankfully done their work and my young son retrieved them as a trophy of an imaginary hunting expedition, to hang above the door of his hut in the wood. That stopped silly visitors continually asking me why there was a pair of horns protruding from the lawn.

It Takes All Sorts

In my youth I had a chum who was fearless. I always thought that no one likes getting hurt. Well perhaps he didn't like getting hurt, but it certainly never bothered him.

If it was more expeditious to do something a painful way, then he did it as a matter of logic, and accepted the pain without complaint. Let me give an example. When he wished to dismount from a bicycle, he would simply set his legs into a walking mode instead of a sitting, pedalling, one. This inevitably resulted in confused entanglement of his legs with the frame, pedals and chain of the bike and usually the crashing of both bike and rider to the ground – although sometimes he would disdainfully shake the machine clear of his feet while staggering to maintain an upright posture. The fact that he initiated the manoeuvre without previously slackening speed made it more violent, but he considered applying the brake an unnecessary waste of effort.

Then again, climbing trees. He acknowledged the law

of gravity in that there was clearly no way of ascending a tree without the vigorous use of arms and legs, and this he did until he reached the very highest point – no less would do. But then he made use of gravity for his return to earth, and in a no less emphatic way than his bicycle dismounting. He merely let go. He took his feet off the branch and relaxed the grip of his hands. Thereafter, absolutely no effort from him was demanded and he flew through the foliage, crashing off branches and hurtling through space until he collided with the ground – a certainty which seemed to give him almost smug satisfaction rather than the alarm which I would have felt. And the funny thing is that I never knew him to get really badly hurt. Often cut and scratched, always bruised (often severely), he never failed to get up and shamble off to the next entertainment.

Perhaps he was so relaxed in his philosophy that he was saving himself trouble that, like a drunk, he impacted more like a cushion than a human body. I have known him dive into the sea half-dressed, not to save anyone but just for a swim. Having removed some of his clothes he didn't bother with the rest so that, when he emerged, he put the dry ones back on over the wet ones and went on his way without a trace of pneumonia. It goes without saying that he became an exceptional rugby player, although I suspect that even rugby was too easy, and he later joined the Royal Marines where he nearly found his niche. I say nearly because he thrived on their assault courses and commando assignments – taking frightful ordeals and brushes with death as matter-of-factly as you and I would take a morning surgery – but you see it was peace-time so he could not really show his metal. I was always sorry there wasn't a war on for him because he would surely have eclipsed Napoleon in fame and achievement.

As it was, having done all the Marines could suggest, he joined his father's drapery business, and later took it over, but the last I heard was that he had retired prematurely due to ill health. It is possible that all his traumata had caught up with him, but I think it is far more likely that a life behind the counter doing nothing more violent than handling fabrics and writing invoices destroyed him.

It takes all sorts, and I never cease to be fascinated. I have already mentioned the deaf lady I stood behind to ask if she could hear me, and she said, 'No', well enough to repeat again today.

Now there is another, not the same, who purchased an anti-snoring pillow from our local chemist. I'm not sure what such a pillow is like or how it works, but the fact is that it is supposed to reduce snoring. When the lady was again in the shop a week or two later our good pharmacist asked her how successful the pillow had been, to which she replied, 'How can I tell? I live alone.'

Mind you, there are some in this fair land who may think that I am not 100 cents in the dollar. I have mentioned before in these columns that I hate killing things, and this applies to those wretched vermin, opossums, which get into my garden and make rose growing and fruit cultivation a farce. Even if I could stomach one, I am not allowed a gin trap because it would catch my wife's cat, so I have a cage trap, baited with suitable foods, and I catch opossums in droves. The snag is then that I have to get rid of them, and while they are not quite in the same category as rats, no one is too keen to see me releasing my opossums into their territory. Well if you knew my neck of the woods you would say there is no problem because I live on the edge of the city, virtually surrounded by millions of acres of fields and rough land, coastline and quarries. Drive out with the cage in the boot, stop at a deserted wild and woolly spot, open boot and cage, and hasten home.

I think it was in my last article that I expressed an empathy with murderers, on that occasion in respect of digging holes for the corpse, and again I must express a certain camaraderie for these hard-pressed criminals because it is incredibly difficult, when it comes to the point, to find a deserted spot in New Zealand. I may go to a patch of arid scrub and, just as I am about to release the animal, up stroll a band of retired master mariners. On a cliff top forty-three miles from anywhere, at the precise moment of opening the boot, seven bus loads of Japanese tourists draw to a halt. A disused coal pit contains an abundance of courting couples who seem to find petting amongst the clinker just the best, while a thousand acre paddock of hay is liberally dotted with people who appear to be there only to stare at me.

The embarrassing thing is, like the murderer, that I cannot give a valid explanation of what I am doing there. At best, I seem to be doing nothing, which is usually interpreted as being caught short and answering the call of nature but when, as has happened on at least one occasion, the very same bevy of spectators see me at two different locales, they have to presume that I am a diuretic addict or else, looking younger than I am, a victim of prostatism. I am a voyeur to the courting couples, and a potential turnip thief to the farmer. I am none of these, but I can't tell them that, so perhaps we should not judge the lady who bought the anti-snoring pillow, without knowing all her secrets?

Dressed to Kill

There weren't many medical students in my year with immaculate evening dress. Only one to my recollection, a character straight out of 'Doctor in the House'.

He was an ex-Spitfire pilot who had inherited a packet from an aunt and was actually chummy with such VIPs as Sir Lawrence Olivier and the late Vivienne Leigh. He could be seen, when embarking on a night of revelry with such notables, to leave the students' hostel not only in white tie and tails but top hat, silk cape with a scarlet lining and swinging a jaunty cane. We loved him for it but I don't think that any of us were envious because we didn't move in such exalted circles. Even a cheap dinner jacket would have looked like gross overdressing at the Saturday night 'hops' that were the high social peaks in our week. A spivvy tie, if I may use the then-current term (am I too far back in the century to keep your interest?), was the acme of smartness at these functions.

However, there was one occasion when it was most necessary for me to have formal suiting and I was up to it. I possessed my late father's evening dress which took the form of dinner jacket and trousers, steely-hard stiff shirts (two), wing collars (three), and black bow tie (one). All these items were of latish Victoriana, early Edwardiana vintage and you couldn't get that wrong when you looked at them on the wearer – any wearer. But to make matters slightly more delicate was the fact that my father had not been quite the same size as me. Nearly, but not quite, and many tailors in Saville Row will tell you that it does make a difference. The greatest handicap was the boiled shirt. Knights of old must have had their armour custom-made and fitted because I can jolly well tell you that anything very rigid which is not the right size is a nightmare both to the wearer and the beholder. Dad's shirts took me in the groin at an angle which called for extreme caution when sitting, while at the same time elevating my chin which was slotted into the wing collar like the head on a chopping block. If I wished to look round, it was necessary to pivot my whole trunk and any attempt to look down was swiftly aborted by that vicious dig in the groin again. Then there was the width ... well having a chest only about two-thirds the breadth of my ancestor did not make for actual discomfort but, to be charitable, the look of the thing was grotesque. My arms stuck out from behind it rather than sprouting from the shoulders, as is the norm, so that I resembled an armadillo posing as a human being. The *pièce de résistance* was the pair of black socks which were impeccable. No one could see that they were too big because the trousers were also too big and concealed the socks at all times bar none ... and the shoes.

I taught myself to tie the bow tie by the simple expedient of persevering tying it around my leg until I achieved some sort of knot which passed muster so long as it stayed tied – something I discovered I was unable to guarantee. If it came undone I required the full services of a large mirror and a lot more time to get it retied. Well, there you have it so far. In summary, a handsome, young, nearly-doctor locked into the sartorial elegance of yesteryear, limited in physical performance by minor details and sweating profusely to boot.

There was more than one occasion when this rig was *de rigueur*, namely the annual Matron's Ball, but such was the nature of this event that the peculiar stringencies of my wardrobe went unnoticed. I think colleagues may recall that many of us became so lubricated at the onset of these balls, and our partners so eager for them to finish, that no one made any great objection to garb as long as it started out looking roughly evening-dressish.

The infusion of vast quantities of cider and cheap Beaujolais (the contemporary 'punch' pre-medication) made me oblivious to the jocular jibes of my friends who were wearing ordinary shirts with studs painted on them and soft collars with droopy, clip-on bow ties. And the passion, not to mention perspiration, of the later night went a long way to melting the stiffness of the shirting in the supra-pubic zone sufficiently to permit more sociable activities than standing rigidly to attention, trying to glimpse the bow tie to make sure it was *in situ* and bow-like. Yes, these thrashes were easy …

The test came one day when I received a gold printed invitation to the twenty-first party of my childhood best chum, one Ian Standingly-Morton – now the Hon. Ian Standingly-M, to give him his full adult title. I hadn't seen Ian for six years or more since our paths parted after school, he to follow in his father's steps as heir to a vast drapery business, I to medical school. Now the worthy Yours Truly was invited to the celebrations at a remarkably swank condominium in Park Lane, West End, presumably hired for the event since their stately home was, I well knew, in Devon. "Formal dress", the card said …

On the night in question I donned the large socks, the larger trousers, I inserted the shirt (to the groin, need I add), slotted the chin into the wing collar and tied the tie. The arms emerged from behind the carapace and I struggled into the jacket. It was raining, pouring. I only had a sleazy 'mack'. I put it on. And took a fourteen bus from Tottenham Court Road to – pause for respectful breath – Park Lane. At 114 I mounted the imposing steps and rang the gilt-plated bell. The door, after a suitable interval, was genteelly opened and there stood a footman in powdered wig and duck-egg blue silk breeches, frilled lace bib, frothy mutton bone sleeves and white satin gloves. Bloody hell! 'Sar?' the creation said.

'Hello', I replied warmly and thrust a wet invitation card in wet gilt at him. He peered at it unwillingly, looked back at my unwaterproofed mack then at the card again, sighed perceptibly and turned, beckoning in the derisory way perfected by the upper lower upper classes. 'Felloe me, Sar.' We trundled along a marble hall to what, by its appointments, struck me as being the ballroom but turned out to be the men's locker room in upper crust society.

'Your …?' asked Lord Fauntleroy, indicating my mack with a searing glance down the starboard side of his aristocratic nose. I wrenched it off as best I could (bear in mind that I wore the suit of armour underneath and so was unable to flex the trunk or neck). He received my rainwear between forefinger and thumb and deposited it rather more ceremoniously than necessary on the floor in the corner in a rather significant way.

'The tie, sar?' This took me by surprise; I didn't think we did a full strip at this juncture. But a glance in one of the twenty-three mirrors around me showed that the knotting was well on the way to needing revamping, something I sensed instinctively would be observed with severity by Silkipants. I said, with a flash of superiority, 'Yes, I prefer the casual knot, Glyndebourne fifty-three', and I was going to add 'my man', but the gut told me that I had pressed my credibility far enough and I might need more later. His look indeed confirmed my hunch but apparently his duties ended there and his union insisted on a co-footman in like silk strides take over – no demarcation disputes in Park Lane thank you.

L. Fauntleroy Mk II beckoned me just as Mk I had done and we were off down the corridors again. Halfway along he paused and said, 'What name, sar?'

Here it is necessary to explain that I may sound stupid but when he said this I was mindful of the fact that here we were in a building absolutely packed full of dukes and earls and the like, probably all having parties of one sort or another. I assumed that footman 002 wanted to know which millionaire's orgy to conduct me to; not even the Sheik of Saudi Arabia owned the *whole* of this lot. So I said, 'Standingly-Morton, The Hon., actually.' To the perspicacious, 002's left eyebrow flickered imperceptibly but, being the good serf that he was, nothing else and we proceeded on until at last we came to a regal pair of ornate doors. We halted, 002 grasped the twin handles of the doors and, with a flourish obviously born of long practice, flung them open simultaneously to expose to my astonished gaze a vast concourse of guests in a this time real dinkum ballroom. Spearheaded by our host, Ian S-Morton, they all looked up at me and my courier who, again practised, chose this moment to bellow in stentorian tones, 'My ladies and gentlemen, pray silence to present … THE HONOURABLE STANDINGLY-MORTON …'

Of Matters Maritime

I had to spend three years of my professional career doing national service in the Royal Navy. We did not get on; I'm just not a 'service' type, saluting and changing into evening dress for supper. Even on dry land your room was called a cabin, the ceiling of which was called the deckhead and the walls bulkheads, and when you went out of the barracks' gates you were going ashore. It was peacetime and the naval hospital to which I was appointed had a large staff and virtually no patients at all. After some months I was moved to a shore base in Cornwall at which I inspected some athlete's foot cases sometimes and then after lunch went back to my wife in our flat in a neighbouring fishing village, the beach in the summer and the pub in the winter. A year of this bland existence and I was sent to sea for a year, during which I spent most of the time seasick and my sick berth petty officer used to have to bring any ill crew to see me lying miserably in my bunk, which usually cured them instantly. After a bit I got dysentery instead, the only person in the ship to do so (always lead from the front, we were told), and had to be landed at the primitive RAF hospital on Bahrein in the Persian Gulf. I and a pilot officer with dengue fever were the only customers and kept piles of stones by our bedsides to hurl at the rats which scampered gaily across the floor. The wing commander, who was senior RAF medico in the Gulf, shared an office with the squadron leader who was CO of the hospital and such was the affluence of British services abroad that they had to share the typewriter, one typing a letter to his CO and then pushing the machine across the table to the other, who would type his reply. It really saved on postage and was very quick; perhaps modern industry could take note of the enormous economies achieved.

After I returned to my ship I was called upon to do the only treatment that I recall in my three years in uniform and that was an emergency appendix removal during a gale so violent that both I and the patient had to be tied to the operating table. I managed to avoid being sick throughout the operation to my, and no doubt the patient's, relief, and in fact spent much of the time trying to keep my petty officer awake, he who was giving the anaesthetic (ether on a gauze mask) with such gusto that every few minutes he would slump forward onto the patient and join him in dreams, whereupon I devised a technique of pushing him back with my foot, out of the fumes, while still operating with my hands, rather like a trick cyclist doing his turn.

A less joyous occasion was when the ship had been rolling heavily all night and the battery of toilets (called heads in the Navy … you see what I mean, surely bottoms would be more appropriate?) had overflowed and emptied into the passageway which, when full in its turn, overflowed into the cabins opposite. One of these was mine and when I awoke in the morning, already nauseated as usual, my bleary gaze over the edge of the bunk fell upon the macabre spectacle of my slippers floating, bobbing up and down in cosy unison with the unspeakable you-know-whats from the loos. Join the Navy and see the sea.

One day the standing orders said there would be a nuclear attack rehearsal, but I was seldom well enough to read such trivial things about the conduct of the ship, and was consequently surprised to find no one in the wardroom for the customary pre-lunch gin. I wandered out on deck to find it all mine; up to the bridge, not even anyone steering although the vessel was chugging along contentedly. It was the Marie Celeste all over again, although of course I am too young to have known the first one. So I went down to my sick bay to see if I still had a petty officer, but as I approached it along the alleyway part of the steel floor of the latter began to rise and in an opening about three inches high I was incredulous to see my petty officer's eyeballs. 'Pssssst' it said. 'What on earth are you doing down there, Ross?' I asked, and he then went on to explain in a histrionic whisper that this was a simulated nuclear attack and that I was supposed to be down there with him and any patients we had, which we hadn't; we never did have. 'Ah yes,' I replied, donning a mantle of superior knowledge which I knew he knew was bullshit, 'but I've been dealing with some simulated casualties. I thought I'd just check to see that you had taken up your correct station for the exercise.' A clever touch, that, which Ross didn't believe either.

Then there was the time in the Mediterranean when I began to suspect that one of our seamen might have typhoid, contracted on a 'run ashore' some days previously. Over forty-eight hours he seemed to be deteriorating and I felt concerned enough to ask our captain how long it would be before we reached Malta where I could hospitalise him. 'About another day, Doc, but if you're really worried we could ask the Chief to pile on the steam.' Which he did and the old ship shuddered and shook all night at a breathtaking seventeen knots until a beautiful dawn saw us under the island's cliffs, where a launch had come out to meet us and convey my patient and me to a remarkable lift up the cliff face and thence direct to the naval hospital. A senior physician met us, examined the man and admitted him for tests and treatment to which he responded well and rejoined the ship three weeks later. In the Navy, the senior medical staff take turns at being the emergency duty man, and it turned out that our man of the day was the senior psychiatrist on the books. It called to my mind the night in Portsmouth when I assisted the duty surgeon to repair a perforated duodenal ulcer; he was the hospital eye specialist, a morose man who regarded me wearily when I cracked the feeble joke that he had not only cured the patient's peritonitis but given him an insight to future health. Well, it was 3.30 a.m.

I didn't leave the Navy under a cloud, I just left the Navy. It happened like this. When the ship returned to the UK for docking and maintenance, I had only three more months to serve, so they appointed another Surg. Lt. in my place and told me to go to the barracks, which I duly did, back living in our Cornish fishing village and taking the bus in each morning, where, in the sick bay, I changed into uniform and sat behind a desk, and occasionally took a stroll around the parade ground to stretch my legs. There were several other doctors appended to the sick bay but no one appeared to notice my existence at all. After a leisurely lunch I would change back into civvies and take the bus home from outside the barracks' gates. On the precise day that I estimated was the end of my three years serving Her Majesty, 3 X 365 less one month's terminal leave, I lunched as usual, changed into civvies, strolled out through the gates and took the bus home. I don't recall speaking to anyone throughout my three months there. That was in 1960 and so far no one has come looking for me. Perhaps the Admiralty thinks I'm still there?

A Specimen Signature

You may not have picked it because of my incredible easy fluency with the New Zealand idiom, cobber, but I am not a Kiwi. I am, in fact, a Pom, although I have lived longer in this country than any other – over a quarter of a century, to be inexact.

I'm not sure, after idly perusing my passport, that I'm not still on a holiday visitor's permit. I therefore decided that it was ripe time to become a citizen of this fair land, if they would have me after a trial period of twenty-six years, and I found my way to a very official-looking government office, where I approached a civil servant behind a counter. 'I wish,' I said to her, 'to apply for citizenship.'

'Where for?' she surprised me by saying.

'New Zealand.'

'Karen,' then, louder, 'KAREN – one for you,' then to me, 'Go over to that counter and wait for Karen.'

I did as I was told; Karen emerged from off stage bearing half a cup of tea (to be pedantic, it was actually a whole cup, half full of tea; I guess you realised that ahead of me).

After my experience with the first young lady, I laid my childish trap easily.

'I wish to apply for citizenship.'

It was too good to be true, because she said, 'Where for?'

'Outer Mongolia.' I've always wanted to be an Outer Mongol. 'You see,' I added, with an earnest look, 'Outer Mongols are taller than Inner ones and I've always wanted to be taller ... because I'm short.'

Karen wasn't very happy about all this, but she gave me a sheaf of forms.

'Fill those in, get two photos of yourself, have a JP sign them as well. If you can't find one we have a man out the back who can sign them all, and bring forty-four dollars,' she machine-gunned at me, and then took a defiant draught from her cup, half full of tea.

'There's just one thing,' I said, beginning to voice a real fear that gripped me, and wishing that I hadn't been so flippant about Mongolia because now she could have me on toast if she wished. 'If I am accepted, do I have to sing the National Anthem and, if so, can it be done with a group of us, or is a virtuoso solo performance mandatory?'

'I don't know what's on at the town hall this weekend,' she said, 'You'll have to ring them yourself.'

I'm glad she didn't understand me because when I repeated this query to a senior official later on he nearly died laughing. However, it was necessary to know, because if a solo was deemed vital, I should have to learn all the words, whereas in chorus I could do what I always do at rugby matches.

Then there was the signing of forms, witnessed by a JP. He said he couldn't read my signature. I said I couldn't read anyone's signature except those of plastic surgeons which are always copperplate stuff. I've often wondered which came first – are they complimented on their writing in primary school and told that henceforth they must devote all their energies towards becoming plastic surgeons? Or is it a fact that once they have become adept at transplanting noses and ears so neatly that they find it is really quite easy to write legibly? On either count I think I would qualify as a brisket puncher at the freezer. Our local chemist says he finds my signature very easy to recognise because he can't read it, at all, and he is not alone.

I recall an episode some years ago in a bank in Tunisia, of all places, when embarrassment gave way to distinct fright if not terror over the matter of my signature. You know how it is when you get your traveller's cheques, always seemingly at the last moment before departure when you have so many other things to do? You have to sign one half of each one then and there, so you tear through them, signing with more abandon and less care than all last week's prescriptions put together, speed signing – streamlined stuff.

So when I strolled into a bank in the capital city of Tunis that day, badly in need of cash but not cramped for time, I duly signed the other half of a fifty in a relaxed leisurely way, presented it to the teller and extended the palm to receive the green. But all I got was a puzzled stare and then a gush of French.

'Sorry, old bean,' I said, speaking loudly like all Englishmen abroad so that he could understand me, 'I never got beyond la plume de ma tante.'

'Votre tante? Possiblement, mais jamais votre plume!'

'Eh?' I replied, in English, with the faintest suspicion that a pun was being made at my expense.

'M'sieur,' he elaborated, 'Ziss ees not your

signature.'

'Yes it is,' I replied smartly, 'I just did it.'

'Pliss do eet again.'

I did. I must admit it wasn't my best and didn't really look like either of the other two specimens my North African friend was looking at before him.

'Un moment.'

He went and got another inhabitant, and they both pondered my calligraphy. They kept looking up at me, as if searching for a mirror reflection in my smiling eyes, now a merest trifle clouded with anxiety.

'Encore, s'il vous plaît,' and a fresh sheet of paper was offered to me. I signed again; and again.

'Non.'

The manager was called, and more sheets of paper. Now I don't know if you have ever tried signing your name more and more carefully, tongue protruding from the corner of the mouth, but if you do, you will produce something akin to a child's printing, which I now did. It was certainly something as far divorced from a GP's signature as it is possible to get. It may be legible for the first time in forty years but it is not you, and this was what quite forcibly struck the manager and his cohorts, whom he now instructed to go and procure a couple of the local gendarmerie. By the time these two gentlemen appeared, I had covered acres of paper with everyone's signature in the world, Hemingway, the Duke of Marlborough and Kiri Te Kanawa being outstandingly clear.

The first thing the police did was ask for my passport, and … there it was, the most beautiful scrawl on earth where I had applied it in great haste under my photo before leaving home. 'There, there you are, there it is, I mean voilà, voilà il est pour vous to see!' I beamed at them.

'Eh bien,' said the police laconically, and sauntered off.

'Formidable, ah formidable,' beamed the manager and returned to his sanctum.

Teller number two left us and the teller numéro uno was left trying to find the original cheque under all the waste paper I had produced.

'Eh, combien? Cinquante, n'est pas?'

'No, fifty please,' I replied.

The Woodpile

My woodpile reminds me of a patient of mine once who was not frankly psychotic but certainly inclined to flights of optimism which were not justified by reality.

He would take entirely inappropriate jobs, such as solicitor's clerk or accountant to an engineering firm, without the slightest knowledge of or qualifications for such occupations – it says much for the quality of the interviewers who took him on.

The story was always the same … a few weeks of swiftly increasing chaos in the workings of the firm concerned, questions asked (too late) and further unemployment. He was, as far as I remember, a bricklayer's mate by trade, so that you can see what I mean.

He did give gold mining, freelance, a go. This was more up his street, but there was no gold where he mined for it. On another occasion, he put on a snappy uniform and hopped up onto the dais before the appointed dignitary could do so to take the salute on a services parade. I began to be fearful that he would award the VC to someone soon.

I'm afraid it was terrible for his wife, who had to be ever on the alert to detect if he had applied for another job such as junior in an architect's office, or assistant lecturer in cybernetics. If he had, she had to dash round and try and explain why they should not take him on, or, if they had already done so (and he really did land some beauts), get him sacked before the first day. This can be a surprisingly difficult task, equally as hard as getting a job, actually.

Sighs of Relief

Well, one day he announced to me that he had turned to writing as a career. This made me sigh with relief because I thought that here, at last, was something safe, that, even if he mucked it up to the maximum as usual, no one would get hurt. How wrong I was. I thought it was even more blameless when he went on to tell me that he was writing a book of jokes. 'You know, funny stories, humorous anecdotes, all clean fun so that it is a family book, pure light-hearted amusement.'

'That's just fine, Les,' I said, 'I hope you do really well; if I hear any good ones I'll let you know so that you can put them in. By the way, won't it take rather a long time to fill a whole book?'

Then came the bombshell.

'Oh, no,' he said, 'I've nearly done that already. I just take them from the *Readers Digest* every week.'

When I muttered in a choking voice about copyright and permission and things, I knew the answer already.

'Oh, I'm sure they won't mind – it will show them how good and popular their jokes are, anyway.'

Bombshell

The next bombshell was that in a matter of days he had completed his book and persuaded a firm to print it, and he actually began peddling it around the avenues for cash, despite my heaviest advices. The inevitable followed shortly after when the legal wrath of the august holders of the copyright in the United States of America descended upon him like a cataclysm.

Fortunately for him, many experts in the field were able to testify that he was not quite psychotic, and he was let off on condition that he destroyed the book and all its copies privately. The printer, scorched but not burnt, delivered them to his house the next day.

The first edition had run to 5,000 on Les's order, but long before he had disposed of the first dozen he had become imbued with such enthusiasm for the project that he had commissioned another 10,000. I went to visit him at home c/o depression and anxiety. Each book was about one-and-a-half inches thick, and 15,000, less a dozen, is an awful lot of books. They were stacked up the drive, on either side, under a tarpaulin; they were filling the kitchen; ditto the spare bedroom; they lined the hall five deep so that you had to progress sideways, shoulder first. Les was in bed in the main bedroom. Well, you could hear his voice, but you couldn't see him until you had crawled through a tunnel of books to the window for air, then sidled along a cleft or gully in the books to his head and arms, protruding from loose books.

'This is a fool's game, this writing business, Doc. I've had enough. I tell you though, it's given me the idea I should have had to begin with. Printing. I'm going to take up printing. And the clever thing is, is what I'm going to print.'

I had to say it. 'What?'
I knew it. 'Money.'

The Sorcerer's Apprentice

And now you want to know why he comes to mind when I survey my woodpile – see opening sentence. I will tell you then about my megalomania, although in all fairness my case is more one of the Sorcerer's Apprentice. You know how it is when you know a chap who knows a chap, and favours get done?

Well, one of my sons is in the farming scene some thirty miles from here and he asked me if I wanted any cheap firewood, because one of his cobbers in his rugby team worked at a local sawmill, and one of his cobbers worked in the transport business and would be coming to town empty to pick up a load of super and so could bring up a load of wood for a nominal sum, that is if I wanted. No one was very interested either way. So I said yes thank you because it just so happens we have one of those new little wood burners recently installed.

For a veritable pittance, the load was delivered. The truck, or rig, as I believe they are now called, was too big to get in our gateway, so it dumped its load just outside. Fifteen tons. Neither could its trailer be brought closer. Another twenty tons. Have you ever seen thirty-five tons of kindling? Stand on tiptoe anywhere in New Zealand and you will be able to see it easily, just to the left of Dunedin. I have calculated that it will take me nearly nine years to cart it up the drive in my ute, and eighty-one years to burn it in our wee stove. I shall be 137 then. Geronimo, I've discovered the secret to longevity.

Leader of the Pack

You'll have to bear with me; we're going back to the good old salad days again. My wife and I were driving into the country the other weekend and we met hoards of motorcyclists coming the other way, going to some rally or other.

The thing which struck me was the sophistication of their machines, huge sleek stream-lined monsters cannoning two people with ease at anything up to 150 mph between the cars jockeying for positions along the motorway, to get there at least two hours before anyone else. Doubtless they started first kick, too.

Here it is: When I was a medical student ... well, I was, once. I was impecunious, but my peers had transport, which made dating by bus rather unattractive, even if said peers only had Vespas and Austin 7s (second hand), and ... motor bikes. So I spent my entire fortune, plus borrowings, on a £30 second-hand motorbike, the key to my social life, the fillip to being, the, the, the ... the greatest disaster of all time.

Apportioning Blame

Mind you, we cannot blame the bike for the whole debacle. I knew absolutely nothing about these things; I merely answered an advert for it, went and passed over my precious loot, and, when the guy had shown me how to start it, I rode it home.

It was a primitive machine, even by those times. It had very few spokes per wheel, by default, and no headlamp. It was incredibly heavy, at 200 lbs plus, yet only a two-stroke of 150 ccs. People simply don't believe that when I tell them now, but I promise you these are the facts.

The end result was a piece of metal which, if it fell over, I had to ask for a bystander's help to right it again. Well, that's for starters. The vices to follow made my name a source of merriment with the local populace, and reduced my cutting edge with the opposite sex to that of a haystack. I hardly know where to start.

At the beginning is a good place, viz, it would not start. The kick-start did not start the motor; there is no point in labouring the fact. Therefore one had two choices, run it downhill and let the clutch in, which was easy if you had a hill handy; if not, one had to push it, which meant running alongside while stoking up speed, and then leaping astride if/when the motor fired, mindful ever of one's desire to have children at a later date in the way one secured seating on the evil thing.

Here I wish to put it to you that this sort of pantomime is fine in a deserted country lane, but if one had been supping with the cronies at the local coffee shop in the middle of the main street, and it came time to go home, with the local township buzzing about, one was involuntarily putting on a free show which many would not have missed for worlds. Frequently I found myself indulging in the ghastly process of running alongside this huge bike, on the outside of the local bus, itself gathering speed, and bearing a row of blankly staring faces watching my desperately twinkling legs and sweating brow, not to mention my manipulations of the throttle, and very likely exchanging bets on when I would be fool enough to let in the clutch.

When I did, one of two things was certain – either the engine failed to fire, and I was swiftly left behind, blowing herniae at every orifice; or it did fire, in which case I found myself running at ever-increasing speeds until that moment arrived when I could safely vault onto the beastly thing. Sometimes this meant that I was running, with gargantuan strides and straining eyeballs, at about 27 mph, before I could get astride, something which I fancy delighted the audience more than a failure to start.

Keeping Cool

Then there was the weather. No one told me that, even in summer, riding bikes is cool, man … but icy. I had no windscreen and, initially, no goggles. I rode with my eyes screwed up, or even shut on cold days, opening them momentarily to see where we were going. This was so hazardous that I had to buy some goggles. These were fur lined – not, I hasten to add, out of quality but because in those days it was the cheapest way of establishing a reasonable seal between the goggle and the wearer. The net result to me was that they steamed up, and I had to keep removing them every half minute in order to see, which was really where we had begun.

The cold numbed my hands to such a degree that,

even when going down to the beach in high summer for a swim with the crowd, I had to wear gloves. Again, the purse would not rise to flash leather jobs, but woollen custom made, knitted by my mother, and for too long it was a source of jocular incredulity amongst my friends that I should arrive on the beach wearing such attire, often plus scarf, and still shivering to boot, for the cooling dip in the ocean, which by then was my very last desire. Better a log fire and a mile run in an overcoat.

Then the rain. Mudflaps were unknown in those days, and I discovered to my chagrin that it only took fifty yards riding the beast in moderate rain for my shoes to entirely fill with water. Not just get wet, but fill, to the top. On arrival at the venue, again that detestable incredulity as they watch you walk from your mount in shoes totally full of water. And if you want to enter someone's house you have to take them off; you can't just walk through carpeted rooms in shoes full of water, albeit slowly leaking and thereby emptying … on your host's carpet.

Decoration Purposes Only

I think I mentioned that the headlamp was only a decoration. The first time I got caught out at night with my motorbike involved a ride of about ten miles home over the moors – no street lamps there of course. So, I borrowed a torch and held it, pointing over the handlebars, in order to ascertain where the road was. Fortunately, in those far off days the density of traffic was nil at night in the rural setting of my youth, but what I had not allowed for was a herd of stray cattle on the road. These wretched animals seemed to take me as their leader, a veritable Moses for the mob, and galloped comfortably alongside me all the way home, even into the urban street where I lived. I put the bike away hurriedly, and was tip-toeing up to bed when my mother called me to the window, 'Come and see all these cows, Boy, there must be something on like an eclipse or something.'

I have mentioned also that the power of the engine was just not up to it. On a level stretch with a following wind, solo, I could muster some 30 mph. With the lady friend on the pillion, not far short of 18 mph. I would wave old Morrises and Vauxhalls past with a gracious gesture, shouting in the slip-stream unintelligible technical explanations about fuel mixture and combustion timing. Alas, when we came to hills, unless they were only a mere slope, the lady had to get off and trot behind. Indeed, on more than one occasion when the gradient approached one in fifty, she was required to push as well. It was not a happy time.

We come to the finale, when it nearly didn't matter about lady friends, then, or for evermore. The petrol tank is between the thighs, even (I think) still in this day and age. Mine was, for sure. It had no gauge – you simply filled up when you thought you were low in juice. I did when I wasn't. 'Two gallons, please', and after the first half pint, the tank was full and the pressure of the pump deluged the whole of my lower torso and legs in petrol. Nonchalantly, I pretended to the pump attendant that I had money to burn and always did this amusing trick. For once the kick-start started, and I rode away into the sunset, the wind on my breeches causing the petrol to evaporate ten times as fast as usual, with, as students of elementary physics will know, a remarkable cooling effect – an instant freezing effect. A breathtaking cryotherapy to any libido which ever considered surfacing. A total Yeeeeaawhow!!!

Doctors in Families

Like me, my grandfather was a doctor, but, unlike me, he lived in an era when one could go on safari to deepest darkest Africa, and that is exactly what he did, in 1871 or thereabouts.

Grandfather Williams was the medical man for a party of eight fairly opulent gentlemen, and took to the whole process like the proverbial duck. Indeed, his tasks were not onerous and appeared to consist largely of shooting gazelle for breakfast, elephant before lunch, and lions in the evening. At other times, he would 'bring down the odd wildebeest, or occasionally a gnu' (he obviously wasn't a David Attenborough fan or he would have known they were the same thing).

He moved among an enormous horde of native bearers who bore an equally enormous quantity of 'quite a good' claret on their shoulders, which was partaken of generously, particularly at the evening meal, to loosen one up, presumably for the lion hunt. On conclusion of which, his genial bearers again rallied to the master, this time with a zinc bath with

India Rubber facings (sic), in which Josiah softened the strains of the day. Mind you, it was a time when the English gentleman was sometimes called upon to demonstrate the mettle which created the Empire, and if the bath water was too cold, or the claret too hot, my relative clouted many a likely person with his jambok (a whip about eight feet long made out of elephant hide) 'to show the fella we can't tolerate that sort of thing'.

However, to prove that he was a man of healing as well, he took along a medicine chest, and was kind enough to list its content for the curious reader of his book. In 1871 this consisted largely of carbolic soap. He must, surely, have had much cleaner patients than we have today. A sop to science and progress was manifest in the inclusion of some quinine, some oil of male fern, and some ipecacuanha 'for dysentery' (perhaps the aim being to desiccate your customer before he had time to get dehydrated from the disease).

JW was undeterred by this somewhat slender pharmacopoeia, and even less so by a total absence of surgical facilities. The local residents of Africa fought many a battle with each other and/or passing safaris to fill in a wet Tuesday, and my relative became adept at philosophising. 'Poor Suleiman was speared today; he crawled into camp trailing his small intestine in the sand from a large abdominal wound. I did my best for the poor fellow, cradling his jejunum in my topi until we reached his hut, where he became quite delirious.' 'Poor Suleiman' succumbed next day, smelling of carbolic, and squeaky clean.

All this, and more, is to be found in his book, which can be ordered, but not obtained, at all reputable bookshops. There is only one copy, as far as I know, and I have it.

What is not related, perforce, is Grandad's own demise, but I have it from the cognoscente that dysentery claimed him, possibly proving in a rather draconian way the indifferent value of ipecacuanha for that, after all. He was buried in Alexandria Cemetery in Egypt for a while, but I gather he was blown up, along with a number of other intending permanent residents, by the mortar shells of the warring factions of the Suez crisis in 1956, an unusual dispersal to an interesting life.

All in the Twist of the Gusset

The patient apologised to me for coming with what he felt was a rather trivial matter, a sore eye, but I replied that I thought the consultation was fully justified, both per se and because eyes were very precious things.

I went on to quote one of my favourites from the great masters: 'Always remember that you can walk on a glass eye but you can't see through a wooden leg.' I knew it had come out wrong but it seemed petty to enlarge on my own deficiencies, so I eyed him fiercely, tacitly challenging him to quibble. I mean, you have to hold the initiative to command respect; I'm calling the shots, and what I say goes. It's called having confidence in your doctor. Bedside manner. Rapport.

It's no good patients hobbling in to see me on crutches if I know their sedimentation rates are down two points; one must show a positive lead and tell them they are now better, whatever mistaken views they may have, and kick their sticks from under them if they argue. Before doing this it is often reasonable to remind them, as so many seem ignorant of it, that 'better' is the comparative and does not mean 110 per cent cured. Then kick their sticks from under them.

Razor sharp

Mind you, as one must continually remind our worthy students, man does not live by bread alone, and good doctoring does not all come from book knowledge. One has to have lightning speed thought processes and razor sharp intelligence to field some of the conundrums which crop up daily in general practice.

The specialists have all the old easy saws like broken legs, infarcts, leprosy, Peutz-Jeghers' syndrome and so forth, all the familiar clinical pictures which make diagnosis and management bubble from the lips without the least exercise of the cerebrum at all, whereas we poor chaps in the field have to problem solve (solving, solving, solving) the whole time, AND with the speed of a computer. It's simply no use scratching the chin and uttering 'Er ... Er ... Er ...'. *They* tend to lose patience and *you* tend to lose patients. One must be bright, original and all confident.

Let me give you an example, a true case history as TV would have it, which occurred only the other Wednesday. This elderly lady came to consult me with the straight-faced story that when she passed wind the cramp in her left foot ceased. What she had come to find out, was the scientific explanation for this? I must confess that even I was momentarily bereft of speech, and I eyed her over the tip of my paper knife, wondering whether to reach across the desk and stab her with it, and afterwards tell the coroner I had slipped while cleaning my nails.

However, my composure returned, and I was next tempted to be facetious and say 'Well done, madam, so all you've got to do now for a cramp-free life is to eat plenty of beans and curry, good day to you. Next customer please.' But such is not my way, and she had after all asked for the *modus operandi* of the treatment, clearly something she believed that we had all been taught shortly after entering medical school, and I was not one to let her down.

Immense wisdom

'Ay yes,' I began, creating an atmosphere of immense wisdom and at the same time giving myself another eight milliseconds in which to formulate a thesis. 'You have made a very perspicacious and brilliant observation. There are not many …' (another fourteen milliseconds) '… people who are blessed with such acute deductive powers …' (note the compliments which never go astray and often help to pave the way for any unforeseen inconsistencies in the ensuing monologue, including cock-ups like walking on glass eyes – and another eleven milliseconds) '… but you are one of them, and you have come across a medical gem which we experts have been aware of for quite some time now.'

Here it might be noted I had created, unwittingly, a slight sand trap for myself; I had begun to outline the chronology of medical discoveries, and she was looking expectantly at me to learn when we had made her discovery. 'It was … it was … in fact … at the time that … when …' (and at this point you will realise that the flash of inspiration had come to me) '… when stockings and suspenders went out of fashion.'

Having become inspired, I was smug enough to sit back for a few seconds to enjoy the perplexity manifest on her brow before going on.

At this point it also occurred to me that perhaps she was pondering (and not all that far from the truth either) whether the demise of the suspender figured so large in my private estimation as to be a date in the history of the planet which would be so vivid in the minds of all as to serve as a more useful reference point than the formal calendar; thus we could have BS – before suspender, a time of hope and anticipation; DS – during suspender, the Golden Age; and AS – after suspender, the wilderness, when nuclear desert went unnoticed.

Scientific drift

But I digress. Whatever she suspected, she was not following my scientific drift and I must explain (thereby also showing that I am a clean young man; well, a middle-aged chap anyhow). 'You see my dear ...' (I now felt quite amicable towards her; what a pleasant old soul she was; how could I ever have thought of stabbing her with my paper knife) '... you see, cramp is due to the circulation not being good enough; the flesh sort of goes cold due to a lack of natural warmth. Now then, stockings and lamentably, suspenders as well, went out when pantyhose came in.'

It all seemed rather obvious to me after that, but her perplexity was still plainly visible, and I was obviously expected to spell it out. 'Well, you see, when you wear pantyhose, and then you blo ... I mean pass wind, the passage of warm air is assured all the way down to the foot, thus remedying the circulation.'

As an afterthought, I went on: 'Don't try too hard lest you blow your foot off,' and I nearly fell out of my chair laughing, until I noticed that she hadn't even blinked and was still fronting the perplexity. Curse and dash it, what had I missed? 'Why, Doctor, does it only relieve the left foot?'

I realised I was toying with the paper knife again. 'Mrs Smith,' I said, and it was time to give clues that the consultation was running into extra time which I did not have, 'Begging your forgiveness for sounding a bit personal, but facts are facts and we medicos don't like to pussyfoot around; a crutch is a crutch, and in the light of the facts as you portray them, there is no alternative but to postulate that you have a twist in your gusset. Good day, madam. Next.'

In the Limelight

My professor always said that, as doctors, we must get used to having an audience – be it the relatives, the public or our peers. Well that's all very well if things are going well. Anyone can act to tumultuous applause and adulation; everyone shrivels up to boos and hisses. It's like wealth: the more it is, the more it is.

At school, my parents made me take piano lessons. For thirteen years I was no good, and I hated it. At primary school I learned the 'Volga Boatman's Song', which had only five notes in it, and, by rote, a piece called 'Sur La Glace à Sweet Briar'. (Being unfamiliar with French at that age, I was under the impression that this meant the Glass was Hard at Sweet Briar, though why such a fact merited a tune escaped me.) At secondary school I was not allowed to play such 'easy' pieces, and was incapable of learning any others. This would not have bothered me a jot except that, once a year, all students of musical instruments were forced to play a solo selection on the stage in front of all the others – and it was a big school. This was a delight to the fluent and a nightmare to the cretins like me. (Which is what I mean about the professor's statement. It's not too bad performing cardiopulmonary resuscitation in front of a gallery when it works. When it doesn't, it takes a certain adroitness in picking the time and words to indicate to the crowd that the show is over, without a dividend. And then there was the occasion at a road accident when I brilliantly diagnosed a fractured femur, and requested a Thomas Splint from the ambulance, and enthralled the mob of hoi polloi by putting it on the patient upside-down. Well, it was a new (to me) folding model, and, being a bit deaf, I didn't hear all the instructions the ambulance man whispered to me. But the great unwashed heard every word.)

But back to the music. I ascended the stage with that feeling in the bowels so well described in the scriptures, set the music on the stand, and, with hands dripping sweat on the ivories, began. Of course it came out all wrong, horribly so, which was as I expected because it always did; but accustomed to that, I plunged on manfully. After about twenty bars (perhaps thirty, I couldn't identify any of them) a voice, which I recognised as the senior music master's, rang out. 'Stop,' it said. I complied, with relief, and was about to rise and gratefully leave the limelight for another year, when it said, 'Start at the beginning again.' This was preposterous, fiendish, beyond all comprehension. I knew it would be worse, and it was. There are many who, having heard the first item, would have sworn that to be impossible, but they were wildly wrong. My plunging fingers produced a cacophony of tortured notes and ghastly chords which defied science. Like a stag rearing in the quicksand, I surged on, dragging everyone down with me. Several of the younger boys in the audience began to shout for their mothers; the school heavyweight boxing champion, accustomed to violent ear problems from his own efforts on the trumpet, not to mention punches in the ring, burst into tears and ran from the hall, while I have it on good authority that a road gang outside with one accord bent down and placed their ears next to the pneumatic drill which one of their number was using, in order to escape the gruesome crescendo emanating from the hall. Though permanently deaf from that day, they all say it was worth it. Meanwhile, on my podium, I stuck with it. Sur la Glace was far behind. They wanted mature stuff, they were getting it. Wagner was nursery lullabies compared to me. I dispensed with the sheet music because I had turned over three pages at once with my sodden finger tips, and anyhow I couldn't read the notes through the sweat of blood and tears. I pressed the loud pedal in an orgasm of destruction, but it was not loud enough to drown the stentorian bellow from the music master. 'Leave the stage AT ONCE,' and, more sotto voce as I walked past him down the aisle, 'For EVER.'

Thus, you see, I became inured to having an audience early on. What my professor omitted to say was that audiences have to get used to me. They never saw the heavy-weight boxing champion again.

One of Those Days

There is a little poster hanging in my consulting room which reads: "I know that you believe you understand what you think I said but I am not sure you realise that what you heard is not what I meant."

This puts it squarely. Hits the nail on the head. It's deadly serious, not funny. I sometimes wonder why I bother to speak in English, though this must partly be because I can't speak any other language. But what I mean is that they always get it wrong. The patient has a backache. 'Lie up on the couch on your back,' I say. At least forty per cent will proceed to lie on their stomachs. I know they are thinking of their backs and expect me to look at the affected region, just as they expect the dentist to look at their teeth when they have toothache, but they give me no credit for subtlety. Mind you, I can be forthright and straightforward and ask a sore throat to, 'Open wide', as I approach with spatula and torch. I never cease to be amazed when some such subjects then open their *eyes* wide. The funny thing is that if you are experienced and, going back to the backache patient, say, 'Lie up on the couch *flat* on your back', you will never get a prone customer. Odd, that one. Another is the chesty case ... you apply the stethoscope to the chest and say, 'Breathe away in your own time through your mouth', to which the genius replies, 'In AND out, Doctor?' I've always wanted to retort, 'No, you stupid git, just in, I want to see how much air you can get in before you burst.'

Then there's the matter of clothes. I have always thought that stripping to the waist meant, by common acceptance if not actually precise semantic definition, removing the clothes above the waist. Added to which, if one is consulting the doctor for bronchitis, heart pain, armpit pain or etc. above the waist, such a request must refer abundantly clearly to the shirtings and singlets. Surely? But no, there is a section of the population who must always start at ground level and work up, and when you part the curtain you find them naked from navel to knees, often with socks still on for modesty. Occasionally there is a lot of puffing and grunting from behind the screens – this usually from old men – and after a quarter of an hour of preparation you find all they have achieved is to get down to shirt sleeves. Thankfully, there are fewer now with braces because a fair percentage of these had reinforcement with string, the knots of which took hours to undo and, if cut, we never had enough string to bridge the gaps when it came to redressing again. Naturally, nearly everyone who is coming for a BP check, and knows it, wears the tightest long-sleeved garment in their possession, even in hot summers.

There are always the individualists and for over a quarter of a century among my clientele has numbered one lady known in my mind as Nudey Hatty. It is a fact of history that, no matter what ailment she comes to see me about, be it ever so trivial, and whatever I say – such as, 'Just slip your shoes and stockings off so that I can see your toe,' – she pops behind the screen and removes everything … except her hat. This is invariably a small black round thing with a rim, like a cup fused to its saucer over which three artificial cherries dangle. Were this not enough, the crowning touch is that when she lies back on the couch and her head rests on the pillow, the latter shoves the hat forward over her eyes, lending her the appearance of a 1930 Chicago gangster's moll auditioning for a now ageing matron's strip club. Naturally I don't make any comment, and it has occurred to me that the lady may be surprised that I do not.

On the whole we are a polite lot, and I have often wondered if the patients would say anything if they were to come into my room and find me dressed in a fireman's outfit, complete with helmet, rubber boats and axe tucked into my belt, stethoscope outside the waterproofs.

Actually, I don't have to try too hard to look silly; fate does it for me now and again. Take last week. Wednesday was the nadir, when I had a fairly new patient in front of me for some diabetic assessment.

'Mr Williams, I'm just going to look at the retina at the back of your eye with this little torch gadget. Please stare straight at that spot of brown on the wall behind me.' 'What spot, Doctor?' I turned to indicate the century-old blemish of gunge which had been my trusty marker over the years. It had gone. An over-zealous new cleaning lady. 'Ah. It's not there. Well, just look at, um, er, well the corner of the picture there.' I peered into his eyeball. The light in the gadget went out. I fiddled with it. On. Off. On, a little. Off. 'Ha ha, need a new battery I think.' The spare in the drawer was an old one I'd forgotten to throw away. Nurse went around to the chemist to buy another while we talked gardening, a subject dear to my heart but not one Mr Williams seemed to know much about. Curious fellow.

New battery, but getting it in seemed to do something odd to the ophthalmoscope because as I began to visualise his retina, the head of the instrument slowly twisted right over ... and then fell off. A glance showed that it was fractured beyond first aid remedy.

'Sorry about that,' I said, 'but we can do that another time. Now I'll take a blood test, just a finger prick and this gadget here will tell us the amount of sugar in your blood.'

These sorts of days are fiendish. 'This gadget here' had never let me down before. I thought for one horrid moment that it wasn't going to do its bleeping. I might have guessed – it wouldn't stop bleeping. A jumble of numbers flashed across the screen and it continued its mayday calls like a miniature burglar alarm gone mad. I tried to put a casual hand over it so that Mr W wouldn't be too disheartened to see the word DEFECT which was now pulsating on the tiny screen but, alas, too late because he asked, 'Does that mean me or the machine?' With heavy but honest heart I had to admit that I thought it probably referred to me.

I sat back in my chair and began to write him a script. Silently I challenged fate to make my pen explode, but it didn't. I have a swivel chair with three legs and once before I had noticed that if one's weight accidentally pitched just a certain angle over the gap where one of the legs was not, it tended to tip. I now fell out of my chair.

RIP

The reader might take a critical view of the patients in my practice, based on my stories, but I hasten to reassure that, at the zenith of my career, I had several thousand customers, and, at the nadir, several hundred less because a) they'd died, and b) the others knew I was retiring soon. What I'm trying to say is that ninety-nine per cent of them were splendid stalwart Kiwis, the salt of the earth, and I would swap them for none. The other one per cent were like the one per cent everywhere: mortals with brain function which would have defied Einstein. Read that whichever way you wish.

I used to dread George's visits to bring us the first of his crop of new potatoes, some two weeks after we had finished our own. He was so proud of his belated achievement, but as well as that he had very poor control of his car and, where he turned it, behind our back door, he invariably put the bonnet right through the hedge, then reversed to put the boot hard against the wall, cracking the mortar. In due course hedge and wall were repaired for next year's onslaught.

One day he rang up:

'Me brother's dead. Can you come and deal with him, Doc?'

He was a pragmatic man, of few words.

I knocked on the front door and entered, as was my custom. There was a dead body lying in the hall, on the floor.

'This is your brother, George?'

'Too true, Doc. That's Gilbert.'

'What happened?'

'He died.'

'Just like that. Did he just fall over in the hall here and … die?'

'Not here, Doc, down at Crown river-mouth; we was down there fishing. I'd thought I had a good bite, and I says to Gilbert I think I've got a good bite and he doesn't argue like usual so I turns round and he's lying there just like he is now, dead.'

'But how did he get to being lying on the floor, here?'

'I brought him, of course; quite a hike heaving him, dead as he was, back two mile to the car, then I put him in the boot as it's lower than the back seat, then back here.'

'But that's thirty-six miles?'

'Yep, but I couldn't leave him there; I couldn't have gone down there again till Tuesday.'

At this stage George was beginning to show signs of impatience.

'Anyhow,' he went on, 'that's what happened so can you get Mr Blackstone out with a box and we can have Gilbert buried by teatime tomorrow; I've got bowls the next day,'

I tried to explain that the national laws do not allow

one to transport bodies hither and thither, however dead they may be, without the express permission of officers of the law or their deputies. And then I said, 'George, there's also the matter of a death certificate. I've never met Gilbert before so I cannot give a death certificate.'

'Why not? He's dead; I can see that, and I'm not a doctor.'

'Yes, so can I, but I have to write something on it.'

'Dead. You can't put that he's alive because he's dead, so put dead.'

Of course the inquest and coroner recorded that Gilbert had died, after much paperwork and bureaucracy, and since there were no daggers sticking out of the body, nor bullet holes, the police lost interest. I often wondered if George would have been a good Prime Minister or dictator, making the laws very simple.

He was, however, one of the few to have the energy and inclination to tidy up after relatives passed on; he didn't leave them on river banks for weekend trippers to, er, trip over.

The Smiths rang to say Dad had Gone, not unexpected since he had been suffering severely with his heart for a bit, so I arrived about teatime at the family home, or messuage, and was shown not into the usual bedroom but the sitting room, where the late Dad was ensconced on the settee, sitting up facing the family, who sat opposite him, facing him.

'We thought he'd like to stay up for tea with us, instead of the bedroom where it gets a bit cold.'

And yet again, the Browns asked for a late evening visit because Dad (a different Dad, you understand) 'didn't seem too good'. Greeted at the door, I was told that this Dad was causing concern because he hadn't sworn much at the tele tonight, 'The programme he always watches and hates.' Well, he was in his favourite armchair, no need to move him from a cold bedroom, but he himself was very cold, very stiff and very dead, so I called the undertaker and the family went on watching the programme he hated, in his memory.

Sparring Partners

You will find that most towns and boroughs have their public works characters who toil away doing all sorts of fairly humdrum jobs, unsung and never fêted.

Indeed, the general public seldom knows their names (although their faces may be vaguely familiar to many), yet the tasks they perform keep the old village ticking over through summer and winter. Being an ex-service type, albeit an unwilling conscripted one, I always think of these worthies as the NCOs of the show, the petty officers of the ship, without whose expertise the edifice would crumble. They are not chiefs or Indians but somewhere in between, with skills and knowledge born of long experience in the field, wisdom and intuition which astounds their desk-driving bosses and is beyond comprehension to their labourers.

Now there was one such, and he a postman, who had been on the rounds all his life. He knew everyone's relatives by their handwriting, everyone's subscriptions, and all the bad debtors. Utterly reliable and honest, he never failed to read a postcard first and he would, with a winning smile, quite brazenly tell the recipient what he'd read to save them the trouble.

He had a great sense of humour and I can't remember when our feud started. I on my rounds and he on his, our paths often crossed several times in a morning and we got to bandying the odd salutation, leg pull, then later taunt, goad and finally abuse and insult at each other. It was childish but fun and it helped to pass the day. I would come out of a house and find a sprig of holly or hawthorn on the driver's seat of my car and, if I cared to look around, I would see the grinning eyeball of Jim peering around a wall or bush to see if I sat on it. Or I might find the ignition keys tucked up behind the sun visor; or an immense pile of junk mail, all the district's advert circulars, stacked up on the bonnet. Naturally I had often been known to hide a sack of the very same when I found my adversary delivering at a distance from his cache, and sit in my car watching and sniggering while he searched for it. A piece of bandage I found was used to tie the pedals of his bike together, and mag-sulph paste made the handlebars a sticky mess to grip.

But I think our best era was the pseudo bullfight which we perfected to such a degree that casual spectators had no doubt that it was for real, and expressed their horror in many ways. The technique was, quite simply, for the occasions when we met, both mounted, he on his bike and me in the car; this I would drive straight at him to try and knock him off. He would take exaggerated evasive action, and try to ram my beautiful paintwork. Actually, it's not as one-sided as you might think. The bike is far more manoeuvrable, with an almost nil turning circle, and can go between lamppost and power poles which the car cannot. The latter has greater speed but can be lured into a no exit, in which case it takes time to change gear and reverse. All in all the fortunes varied fairly equally, and although I never actually did physically knock Jim off, there were times when he knew that the shots were called against him, and just before the moment of impact, as he mounted the pavement with me an inch, no more, behind him, he would leap off his machine in a splendidly theatrical way and crash to the ground, or into a hedge, shouting vile abuse as I hurtled past, crowing mercilessly at the vanquished from my chariot. Locals who were in the know used to watch the charade with some relish. It gave many a weary housewife pegging out the washing a wee break in her morning. Foreigners and strangers were aghast, took my number and phoned authority, or just vowed never to settle in our neck of the woods when it was explained to them that that was how the postman and the doctor generally behaved. Well, small things ...

Came the day I was away and I had a locum who was very much my stature and colouring, I had to lend him my car. You've guessed it ... but it was good while it lasted. He was sitting in the car outside the post office reading the mail, when Jim emerged from the building ten yards behind the car and espied whom he thought was me. Many have described what followed. The light of battle gleamed brightly in Jim's eye as he wheeled his bike up behind the car. He took the sack of mail off, placed it on the road, and then suddenly threw the bike onto the roof of my car (luckily it sported a roof rack at the time). With a wild whoop, he leapt onto the back bumper of the car and began to jump up and down like a demented chimpanzee, voicing a diatribe with fierce glee, as he rocked the vehicle and its astounded occupant up and down and side to side. After a brief interval, the shaken locum emerged to confront his tormentor, whose face, we are told, was the picture of the century. He paused only to gasp 'Bloody HELL', before snatching the bike and jumping on, to pedal off at speed to the far horizon, leaving the sack of mail sitting in the middle of the road.

Nelson Meets His Waterloo

This is really part two of my portrait of our excellent and esteemed petty officers of the borough council, not that the postman worked for the council but you know what I mean.

This relates to a gang of chaps who seem to have a lot to do with water supplies and drains and pipes and cables and holes in the road. Sometimes they plant trees but nearly always they are digging them up. They have hearts of gold, lungs full of nicotine and hollow legs. They know where every underground service is without any reference to maps or charts and they can daintily dig holes in pure solid tarseal with the tip of a shovel as effortlessly, or so it looks, as you or me cutting sponge cake.

They get called, usually from the pub, at all sorts of dreadful hours, usually in the very worst weather, because that is when most of the drains block. And they are led by a foreman called Nelson (I think it is a coincidence that England's famous sailor had the same name, but I'm not sure because they were both of the same sterling breed, men of metal, which shows mere mortals like me up as being pretty putty-like).

The grand blockage

Well, the tale I tell was just such a night, when the gates of the heavens had opened and the rain had descended in feet, not inches, and all the storm water had flooded into the sewers which, I gather, is a great no-no in urban plumbing circles. You just can't mix the pure with the poos, if you see what I mean.

Ultimately the dawn dawned, but somewhere around predawn a Grand Blockage had occurred. While there should have been great volumes of water sloshing down towards the sea and many happy local residents pulling their toilet chains and contemplating a happy hygienic day ahead of them, there was neither. The pipes in the lower part of the town were dry, and the residents were far from happy as they contemplated an overspill effect in their smallest rooms. And indeed it got worse as manhole covers in the upper suburb were lifted by unseen forces from within to disclose the very visible, and even more vividly odorous, contents beginning to dominate the world above.

So enter the gladiators, Nelson and his men, shambling along the road from their ramshackle truck. The inexperienced eye might have thought there was an air of apathy, even an idleness, in the way they slouched, taking their time and using a more than measured tread. The vile stub of cigarette that always smouldered at the left-hand corner of Nelson's mouth seemed to epitomise the leisure that was so inapt when the population needed saving in a hurry.

To me, and others like me, though, this stinking fag was reassuring. We had never seen Nelson without it.

It was always smouldering – we presumed it did so all night while he was asleep. It certainly always did so while he drank beer, and had he turned up without it, or with it long and clean and burning sweetly, I should have been alarmed and begged him not to start until the norm had been re-established. No, here I saw Sir Francis Drake before me, confidently finishing his game of bowls before routing the Queen of Spain's Armada.

And so it was that Sir Francis, the erstwhile Nelson Bogworth, cast his eyes slowly about, grunting occasionally and sniffing often. You couldn't actually see the stratagems piling up in his brain, but you knew that this is what was happening; this human computer was taking in all the gradients and pipes and road bends and terribly complex calculations, all spiced by the fumes of nicotine which drifted up from his stub into his left nostril. Finally he took his shovel and applied the tip to a section of tarseal, a taciturn man this, and his cohorts began to dig.

The coup de grâce

Finally the hole was dug and, sure enough, at the very bottom, some eight or nine feet below us, there was a jumble of broken pipe. The diggers eased back. All eyes turned to the maestro who majestically lowered himself into the hole and began to accomplish the *coup de grâce*, as was his privilege as leader of the pack.

Well the *coup* was indeed *grâce* (in fact *gros* would be the *mot juste*). If I may use history again and this time bring in Samson for my analogy, Nelson knew just the right spot on the right pillar to bring the temple down in one. He unblocked the blockage with one movement, but, like Samson, he made no allowance for the fact that he was still *in situ quo* and that nature was about to overtake him with an awesome certainty and in a uniquely dreadful way.

The entire pent up wrath of several streets of sewage was released in a trice and its headlong tidal wave engulfed our hero in a ghastly flood of nameless blackness. For a few agonising seconds we thought he was gone and our ears were deaf to the distant roar of cheers from the residents uphill of us, whose lives were now cleansed of the frightfulness.

However, like the late admiral, and unlike Samson, our foreman was not gone, just temporarily ablated.

As the evil morass fell rapidly in level in his hole, the top of his head emerged, then his eyes, which were shut at first but soon opened to reveal startling whites like the coloured minstrels of yore, then the rest of him – well, down to waist level at least. There it seemed the level would stay, but we cared not, safe in the knowledge that our admiral was still among us.

But then there was a sort of a gasp from someone, and we all peered at him again, and the silence was palpable. A sort of awe emanated from us, a tangible reverence if you like. At last a voice, braver than most, spoke out. 'Coo, Nelson, yer fuckin' fag's gone out ...'

The Zap Presentation

You know these drug firm evenings, where we all go along and have some refreshment at a local hostelry and then sit in deep chairs and snooze while someone bashes NSAIDS for the trillionth time, and tells us that they can upset stomachs? Well, I have become so weary of 'learning' the same information (only NSAIDS, ACE inhibitors, and asthma medication ever seem to be presented in our fair city, but *fortissimo*, sometimes three in a week) that I have to admit that I now often prefer to snooze in front of the TV, which shows much the same sort of programmes but in the comfort of my own home. Thus it was that, when I did recently elect to go and hear what was being said about arthritis and its therapies at the currently in vogue venue, a luxury block of motels, conference rooms and swimming pools, I found I knew very few of my colleagues present. I hadn't been for so long that all the new young GPs were strangers to me (after all, I am so very old now, at fifty-four, that they are my sons' peers).

I entered, and my hand was gripped by the lead

rep – I don't know many of them either, for much the same reason, but clearly my fame had gone on ahead, for he evidently knew me well.

'Glad you could come! Lovely to see you!' he beamed. 'Come along in; have a drink!'

Armed with a glass, more serious chit chat.

'And how's the wife? Good, good. And the children? Splendid, excellent. Have you met FRED? This is FRED. Now, how about the President, come and meet him.'

I was propelled through the crowd, seeing only one I knew, Hugh Basham, propping up a pillar, staring into an apricot juice because he is almost stone deaf and a teetotaller, so I gave him a cheerful nod, and was then having my hand pumped by a silver-haired patriarch. 'Nice to have you here, splendid to see you. Have another drink. Gerald – get him a decent double this time, it's been a long time, I forget now, which is your neck of these woods?'

I told him.

'Of course, of course, dashed cold spot out there in the suburbs, have another whisky. And how's the little woman? And the kiddies? Good, good, good. Ah, here's the film.'

We were to see an audiovisual on the subject, so we all sat, and watched some statistics, some diagrams, graphs and, surprise surprise, some real live arthritics warming their aching joints in various contrived postures in front of a large variety of heat lamps and warmth projectors. Their frowns before, and smiles after, could be called anecdotal evidence by the cynical, but, unhappily that is often par for the course in these presentations in my experience.

Then we all broke up for more drinks and a substantial buffet meal, and I was just immersing myself in seafood, to which I am inordinately partial, to the exclusion of conversation, when a young man approached me.

'Excuse me, but which neck of the woods did you tell the C-in-C you worked in?'

I told him.

'But that is my parish ... '

'Well,' I said, 'I've been there for twenty-five years and to be honest I've never seen you there. Have you just come?'

To my surprise, he turned on his heel and was gone. But not for long. Just as I forked another five giant prawns into my face, he reappeared, rather like one of those instant ghosts that are so technologically easy to produce on the screen these days.

'Doctor,' he said, 'you are at the wrong conference. This is the Zap Home Fire and Heater Company Annual Meeting. I believe yours is on the mezzanine level.'

I collared Hugh, who was toying miserably on his own with chicken legs au Sauvignon, and we belted past the President, past FRED, and Gerald, and the rest. 'Regards to your wife and the kids,' I think came from Arthur whom I had never set eyes upon until that instant, and we were gone into the night.

Well, not quite, actually, because on the way down to the mezzanine we passed the Circular Tyre Company's monthly evening, and a wicked thought came to me. 'And how's the better half then? Haven't seen you for ages.'

But no, honesty prevailed, and we went on and slipped into our seats at the back of our own, medical affair. The film was just finishing, and the guy in front of me yawned, and said, 'A bit anecdotal, if you ask me.'

Anyone for Tennis?

People might be tiring of my accounts of social gaffes, England, mid twentieth century, rural middle (trying for upper) class. Not nearly as much as me.

OK, this one: THE TENNIS DANCE (I nearly put BALL) of the SEASON, Budleigh Salterton, Devon, circa 1950? – somewhere around there (which is what circa means).

Let it be known I am not and never have been, a tennis player, but living where I did, when I did, and being a public school boy (senior, by then), I was, de rigueur, part of the summer tennis tournament scene, albeit only watching the girls' matches, for two weeks before the awarding of prizes and the dance at the CLUB.

I bear no malice towards the male tennis players who ultimately and inevitably partnered the female ones at the dance, whether victors or vanquished on the courts. Doubtless the 'après dance' levelled it out, regardless of prior scores such as 'fifteen love', 'thirty love' or even 'love all'. These chaps played for it with muscular energy, while I languished at the bar with a shandy (I was about seventeen then). But come the dance and I really had to have a partner. You can't dance with a glass of shandy and still be respected in the coffee shops of East Devon.

As luck would have it, a lady friend of my mother's had a French au pair (as they later came to be known) staying, in fact a rather delectable lady indeed, and, to cut a SHORT long story short, it was arranged between the four of us that I should escort her to THE OCCASION.

But here it all starts to go wrong, badly wrong. Monique's English was non-existent, and, by signs and gestures, we devised that she had no long frock this side of the English Channel and would therefore have to make do with a short cocktail job. She certainly had the legs for it. So I, in order not to embarrass her, could not wear my late father's Edwardian evening dress, but attempt what in fact was a frightful compromise viz a dark blue pinstripe suit surmounted by a vulgarly flashy yellow and mauve bow tie, the epitome of bad taste in that it was clip on, to boot.

The evening endured a gruesome start when the exhaust pipe and silencer fell off my mother's elderly Austin, which I had borrowed, en route to the club and the French lass beside me began to scream louder than the engine noise, even unsilenced. At the venue and throughout the evening my peers and rivals brazenly looked askance at my sartorial disaster, magnified by the fact that Monique had, after all, in fact, indeed, actually, dammit and blast it, what English don't you understand? turned up in a full ball gown. And me in …

But finally I went to the men's room for a tidy up, and in the mirror came face to face with the ultimate in sandbagging – my ghastly clip-on yellow and mauve bow tie was (and probably had been ever since the debacle of having to salvage the exhaust pipe and silencer from under the car) hanging vertically by one clip only from one wing of my shirt collar.

I haven't been to many Budleigh Tennis Club dances since then. Very few. Well, not one that I can remember. In fact I can only remember the one I wish I could forget.

Concrete and Home Brew

Before I came to New Zealand, very many years ago, I was serving in one of Her Majesty's ships, coincidentally in the Persian Gulf, which, in those days, was very different from the present scene; there was nothing going on at all, so that, between mouthfuls of gin, we used to chat.

After about eight months of this stimulating existence, the conversation had reached such fever pitch that I had told the captain that I intended to emigrate to New Zealand when my commission ended, and a few months later he replied with the extraordinary information that he had once been seconded to the Royal New Zealand Navy for a couple of years, and, from his experiences here, he thoroughly endorsed my decision. 'One thing, Doc – make sure you've got a good mixer.'

In the context, I assumed he was referring to the means of blending the tonic with the gin, and was beginning to reassure him that that would be the least of my problems, after so much practice in the Service, when he enlightened me.

'No, no; concrete mixer my boy. Concrete. Everyone in New Zealand has a concrete mixer. Can't get by without one. Back breaking stuff mixing it by hand. Takes hours. Must have a mixer. Take my tip, get a good one right off, and new too, not second hand; you'll want it to last a lifetime.'

'Gosh, sir,' I said, 'thanks very much for telling me. Er, what do I do with the concrete when I've mixed it?'

Sore thumb

'Make paths. Paths. All Kiwis spend all of every Sunday morning making concrete paths. You'll stick out like a sore thumb, a real Pom, if you don't make paths every Sunday. Anyhow, if you don't make them, your neighbour will want to borrow your mixer, and if you haven't got one, well ...' His voice trailed away, but I could see the ignominy and degradation which would be my fate from the twist of his nostrils.

This mixer was a must, and I felt a smouldering sense of resentment that neither the brochures nor New Zealand House had made any reference to such an integral part of my projected new life in the Antipodes. Take a new car, they said, and eat ice creams at half-time in cinemas, but not a hint of concrete and its creation.

The captain had been drinking while I reflected thus, but he broke in, voicing his own reverie.

'And founds.'

Perhaps the gin was eroding his syntax.

'I beg your pardon, sir?'

'Founds,' he said again in a tone of fond nostalgia.

'As well as paths, you make founds in New Zealand,

usually on Saturdays, all day.'

'What are founds?'

'Doc, I have to confess that I never really discovered. I never had one of my own, and I was recalled to the UK before I could make one and work out what I'd do with it. The fact is, I used to be asked to go around to a friend's place to help make founds, lots of us would go and help anyone who wanted it. The point was a lot of concrete is required in rather a short time, more than for paths, and we'd shovel and mix and pour and float and shovel and mix and etc. etc. all day at great speed. It was very tiring, especially if it was hot and sunny, and we had to drink lots of home brew to keep going.'

Being still then very much a Pom, I said: 'What's home brew?'

'Beer made at home, of course.'

'Why is it made at home? Why not just go and buy it?'

'Well, you could buy it, of course, but then what would you do with all your home brew? You see, Doc, at all times when Kiwis aren't mixing concrete, they make home brew. It's very important. It uses up a lot of bulky old containers which would otherwise just be cluttering up the place. Like old concrete mixer bowls, for instance.'

Almost forgotten

I could see the logic of this, and nodded wisely, resolving to visit the library when we reached home port to brush up on the subject of fermentation as well as cement. Of course I did neither in the event, and the captain's advice languished at the back of my mind, almost forgotten, until a year or two later, when I was on the verge of leaving the UK for the Big Adventure, and I chanced to meet a colleague who had just returned from being a locum in New Zealand.

We talked of this and that, and it was all very jolly and most informative. Suddenly, he said, 'One thing I really learnt, and you might not believe this, but in a hundred years in England I would never have been aware of the difference between fat and sharp sand. And the selection of aggregates – well you'd never believe it.'

At first I thought he had been reading the fine print in the *British Medical Journal*, but suddenly a bell began to tinkle at the rear of the brain.

'You are not, by chance, referring to making concrete are you?'

'By Jove yes, and block laying. There's simply nothing to compare to a perfect six to one, not too wet, you understand, neither too stiff, so that she just floats beautifully, and if you ...'

'Jim', I interrupted, 'Jim, I think I know, and I'm going to get a mixer, a new one, as soon as I step ashore, but tell me one thing, what is a found?'

'I don't know. I only helped with three founds and on each occasion it was very hot and sunny and our host gave us some putrid fluid to quench our thirst with and later on it seemed terribly funny and we didn't do any more to the found and fell asleep.'

Like a dream

I still have my concrete mixer. It cost me £64 brand new in 1961, on arrival here, and it still goes like a dream. My neighbours borrow it occasionally. I use it about once a decade.

I loathe and detest making concrete, and, when I do,

my peers cry with mirth at my boxing, which requires the concrete to hold it up. Very often I find it simpler to make the concrete so stiff it stays up on its own, with an occasional patting with the hand by me to restore a sag or bulge to approximate to the intended shape.

I made home brew once, twenty-seven bottles in the brew, and I was so seriously and dangerously ill after drinking the first half glass of the first bottle that I forsook home brew thenceforth. That apparently means that I can't undertake a found for fear of dehydration, thank God, and anyway, in twenty-nine years to date, I have only so far completed one and three quarter metres of path.

Breaking and Entering

Breaking and entering is something most GPs have to do, from time to time, in the course of duty – or that has been my experience.

I think I mentioned once before how I fell through a crumbling window frame into a patient's bath, to be clobbered on the head by the owner. What has often struck me, in a less literal sense, is how easy it is to break in without apparently arousing the curiosity of the neighbours, and certainly no one has ever attempted to stop me.

There was the time when someone rang me and said Old Charles' papers hadn't been taken in, and they hadn't seen him around for days. So I went round there and cased the joint, as I believe other expert 'breakers-in' put it. The said joint was locked up but through the bedroom window I could see the elderly Charles lying motionless on the floor wearing only a singlet. We had had some icy weather around then and the very spectacle made me shiver, but I wasted no time in breaking the window and easing myself in. To my surprise the venerable old stick was still alive, but very cold indeed. In fact he was rigid, and I found to my amazement that I could lift him off the floor simply by lifting his head in my hands, rather like those hypnotised people you see on the stage lying horizontally between two chair backs. In fact this proved very useful because when I summoned an ambulance, it proved very difficult to get a stretcher into the old house, so narrow were its doorways and corridor. So we passed Old Charles out through the broken window, draped with a towel for modesty, but otherwise without artificial stiffening, to be placed on the stretcher outside. To me this constituted an amazing spectacle, but the locals never took a second glance.

On another occasion the patient herself rang me up at nearly midnight and, while describing her symptoms, fell suddenly silent and then very audibly fell with a thud to the floor. With piercing perspicacity I deduced that something was wrong and in due course (about ten minutes later) I was casing her joint. She lived alone but in this case her windows were far too high up to see in. I ascended the flight of steps up to the front door – a plate glass, locked door – through which I could see my erstwhile caller lying on the floor, gesturing, but hampered by a very evident hemiplegia. Now this, I thought, was a real burglar's nightmare. No sticking brown paper to the glass with toffee and giving it a gentle thump with the fist. A tentative kick only badly dented my shoe. There were no crowbars lying around. Not even a garden tool. I went back to the car and cast around, and there it was. It was the dinosaur era when cars had starting handles. I had to use mine often so it was always at the ready, a nice solid steel bar with a bit of weight. I tapped it on the glass door; I hit it a bit harder; I swung it fairly heftily; I tried an upswing as if to hit a six; I biffed it very hard indeed. I might as well have been using a feather. I stared through at the lady on the carpet again to see if I could determine, from her expression, why she might have bullet proof glass for a door. She stared back and again gestured hemiplegically. I nodded and mouthed reassuring lip movements at her, waving my starting handle to show how resourceful I was and that help was at hand, but a look of terror started into her eyes.

I went back to the car to see if time had been able to generate a more effective instrument. Well there was the jack, another weighty bit of metal, and I conceived the idea, as David did so long before me, of increasing the hitting power by tying the tow rope to it so that I could use it like a sling at my Goliath, that bloody door. At least this time my patient's face showed bewilderment rather than fright, as I approached with my infernal device. Dave must have been practising with his to get such a sweet shot in first time whereas when I worked up enough centrifugal force to, I hoped, crack the glass, I let go in the wrong segment of my swing and the jack went arcing off into the night, trailing the tow rope behind it like a rocket with a hemp tail. Seconds later there was the unmistakable sound of it passing through someone's greenhouse. My patient caught my eye, unhappily, and I essayed a reassuring gesture – I mouthed 'Don't worry', and tried a sickly smile, then realising again that I was empty handed, I showed her my hands, felt even sillier, and then nodded as I was fast running out of gestures. It had to be the starting handle again. I mean, dash it, the night was beginning to wear on a bit, and this was turning into a farce. I began feeling immense sympathy and not a little respect for the perseverance and pure commitment that full-time burglars need to make a steady crust. Swings and roundabouts – I expect there are some very easy ones like Old Charles, but there were obviously those that made you earn your loot. So, with the sweat of desperation breaking out on my brow, and whirling the starting handle like a dervish, I charged the door for the last time. The sheet of glass imploded with a thunderous report, to be followed for the second time in five minutes by the sound of millions of shards of glass raining down on hard surfaces and a howl of terror from my rescued patient. I rather fancy that, in the heat of the moment, a cry of Geronimooooo had escaped my lips.

And through it all, not a light went on, not a neighbour stirred. Next time I think I will get one of those huge articulated trucks and have the whole house removed to hospital. Nobody will notice.

The ambulance man made only passing comment. 'What a lot of glass there is on the floor.'

'Yes,' I said. 'The door must have slammed.'

'Must have been quite windy out here then,' he answered, 'because we passed a greenhouse down the road which is a write-off – not a pane of glass left in it.'

Changing Times

Times are changing. There was the era when, during those harrowing sessions with one's accountant, I would be staring owlishly at a series of figures on the piece of paper in front of me and suddenly, impatiently, he would lean towards me, cast his eye over the numbers (upside down to him) and immediately come out with the total, plus a decision, from within his amazing brain.

Now he – a descendant of the original he – cannot do this, or if he can, he keeps it a well-veiled secret. The modern version lives and breathes by means of a calculator. Ask him how he is and his immediate reflex action is to press three digits on his calculator, glance at it and say, 'Fine thanks.' In fact, I envy him his total faith in the machine. I have one, a very poor cousin to his exotic model (which I suspect does calculus given only your birthday and the phase of the moon to work with), but I can never be sure I've pressed the right buttons and spend enormous amounts of time checking the result it gives me with a pencil and paper. Sometimes it is correct and sometimes not, which doesn't help me at all.

Then there's the newfangled fax machine. I didn't know it existed until I was paying a visit to my insurance company one day and there was a query which could only be answered by head office in Wellington. 'We'll fax it up to Wellington,' said the mature matron behind the counter. (Actually, not being familiar with the word, I did wonder if I had heard correctly, and gazed at her with some astonishment, thinking perhaps she had done time in one of the rougher services before joining insurance and the patois had stuck with her – possibly I should reply in like ribaldry, but a small voice somewhere within me told me to only nod, so I did.)

With evident pride at the new toy, she switched it on, adjusted knobs, fed in our query, pulled levers and watched. There was a degree of activity from within the machine, some whirring and clicking while it digested my prose, and then a period of silence. I stood on one foot; and, after a while, the other. I leaned on the counter and pinched my nose reflectively. 'Someone in Wellington will have to read it and reply,' the lady said, clearly sticking to polite words this time. I folded my arms, and idly mused on what a crumby summer we had last year.

Time passed. I stole a look at the 'faxeress', thinking how absurd I had been to think she had been a fish wife. Morning tea approached. 'Do you think,' I asked politely, 'that there is anyone in Wellington?' I didn't want to imply that her new device was faulty. Equally, I have often wondered anyhow if there is anyone in Wellington, which is why I put my question as I did. 'Well, I don't know,' she replied, 'But there is no doubt that the message has gone off.' 'Quite so,' I replied, 'But it is really only the answer coming back that interests me. Could you let me know when it does, because I must get on with some work now.' By next day the reply still hadn't materialised on the magic machine, and, exasperated, I requested the company to try using another scientific device called a T-E-L-E-P-H-O-N-E.

Well times do change, and one has to try and keep up, but so often it takes you by surprise. Not two days later I was conducting my rooms and the gentleman consulting me was saying how depressed he felt, and how he found it increasingly difficult to get on with those around him, and what could I suggest. Naturally I was relieved to find his blood pressure slightly elevated, giving me a handle to work with, and when I was done, I wrote out a few requisition notes – chest x-ray, bloods and the like.

'Get these done and then come back and see me next week; I'm sure I'll be able to help you.'

'Oh I can't do that, Doc.'

'Why not?' I queried.

'Well, I'm in prison.' Like with the fax maiden, I wondered if I was awake. He said it just as I would have said I was on holiday. This was Butler's Erewhon, live, in colour.

'Forgive me asking, I know I'll kick myself the moment you tell me, but if you are, ahem, in, well, prison, well why, or rather, how, I mean, here you are ...' I simply had to drop my voice to a low tone, 'I mean, have you ... escaped?' I shot a glance out of the window, half expecting to see warders approaching along the footpath, and suddenly yearning for my nurse to ring through to tell me that the hospital pharmacy was on the phone yet again to dispute my scripts for Isogel by the hundredweight; but no such luck.

Anyhow, my convict replied impatiently, 'Nar, come

off it, Doc, it's me day off. Yer don't think we stay there *all* the time, do yer?'

Incredulous, both of us, for diametrically opposite reasons. 'Well, no, of course I don't, no naturally not, yes, days off, like nor … er like us, I mean, dash it. So um, when could you come again. Do you get every Tuesday off?' Adding with a flash of brilliance which went sour even as it left my lips, 'I can understand why you get depressed with those around you.' He settled for getting the x-rays and tests done in three months, and coming back for review and therapy in six months.

My sister had rather the opposite experience. At the time, she was living just outside London near a rather classy golf course on the fringe of which she was wont to walk her dog, and was thus doing one afternoon when a small car drew up and out got none other than Her Majesty Herself – with her corgis, which she proceeded to walk towards my sister. We are, perhaps, an old fashioned family with, perhaps, quaint awe of the monarchy and my relative became all agog if not totally legless at this impromptu meeting with The Top. She recalls to this day that she was in a mental turmoil as to whether she should curtsey, or say 'Good afternoon, Queen Elizabeth', as to the vicar, or get trendy with a 'Hi, Liz'. ('Nice to see you, Mrs Windsor' actually flashed through her demented thoughts). It being summer in England, she was wearing a heavy rain coat and gumboots, and, if you think about it, these are not the ideal for a sartorially elegant curtsey, so she eschewed that one and settled for a goofy smile and a totally idiotic flexion of the neck, as if being inspected for hair mites. To prove that she hadn't been dreaming, a few yards further on she bumped into the bodyguard who had escaped her attention until then, and these rather stern-looking worthies regarded her bizarre posturing with not a little alarm, but they let her go untroubled, although they stood and watched her all the way to the bend in the road, just in case.

The Sands of Time

My father, long since passed to that Greater Surgery Up There, bless his soul, never learned to drive a car nor even ride a bicycle, although he was around for all of the first half of this century.

This may seem remarkable to many of you who, like me, were alive in the 1930s and know that cars and bicycles were really very common even then. Not like one of my sons who recently remarked that a certain film on TV must have been prehistoric, *viz* pre-1960, 'because there were no white lines painted on the roads'???

Well, anyhow, the reason that the OM was so lacking in skills which we now take for granted was that he didn't need them. He was, in fact, attached to the British Colonial Service in Egypt for much of his working life, and his duties as MOH required him to travel vast distances across the trackless wastes in a very wild and woolly area, from Cairo southwards to the regions of the Upper Nile and as far as the Sudan. For these journeys the only mode practicable was the camel, and so Father became an expert on that most uncomfortable and vicious beast. Apart from its habit of biting its passenger whenever it can, it ambles and, when goaded sufficiently, runs with a gait which you may not have studied but if you do, you will perceive at once that it uses both legs on the same side at the same time, if you see what I mean. Let us try that again. It advances both right legs simultaneously, and then both left ones. Got it? A lurching business which easily dislodges the inexperienced, especially as it gathers speed, but the more disarming and perhaps more unexpected result is that this motion very soon produces seasickness in the rider unless one has a stomach of iron. I have not, and my admiration for my relative, covering hundreds of miles a month on this dreadful animal long before maxolon had been invented, is unbounded.

I suppose that undoubtedly he became used to it, so that it was not so bad after the first 5,000 miles, but therein lay his undoing, for the more mechanised world awaiting him on his retirement from this desert endurance test is sparsely populated with camels, working ones anyway, and the niche of Devon near Torquay where he finally alighted had none at all. By that time and age he had become somewhat inflexible, I think, because he shunned even trying to drive the car which he bought for my mother and was content to sit at her side uttering phrases in Arabic roughly translated as, 'Get going, thou vile beast of Hades' when the car wouldn't start (this, I hasten to add, directed at the car rather than at my mother … I think).

Apart from the car not trying to bite him, I believe he certainly would have preferred a camel since it had so few, and at times no, moving parts to go wrong. Finally came the war, and with it petrol rationing and the withdrawal of private cars. At this, Father visibly sneered. 'That's what you get for total reliance on mechanical things,' he gloated. All Eubulus (his favourite beast) ever needed was some dried thistles and four hundred gallons of water a month. So we took to bicycles ... but not Dad. He walked. Everywhere. Well that is a very commendable way of getting around, and much approved of in these cholesterol-conscious days, but it has to be emphasised that it tends to be a solo effort, and loses something when everyone else is cycling to the venue. I think what I am saying must be dawning on you.

Consider picnics; they are not things you usually have on your doorstep; you go places and eat in the wilds, that's the fun of it; but if one of you is walking there while the rest of you are biking, either he has to set off about four hours before everyone else, or else he arrives at the spot on the moors just as you are picking up the hard boiled egg shell pieces and rinsing out the coffee flask in the stream, prior to pedalling home.

One had to get used to taking all this in good part, since nothing on earth would change him, and I often wonder if it was this mild eccentricity that imbued my mother with a penchant for the most curious practical jokes, as a sort of reaction to her forever-ambulant husband, he spending the whole of his latter years either getting there or getting back again. For whatever reason, Mother began inoculating chocolates with mustard and cayenne pepper and then offering them to her guests at card parties, all the rage in those days except (soon) Mother's. She would guffaw with ill-concealed mirth at the antics of a victim, now beset with a palate on fire and a blazing tongue, and laugh off the threats mumbled through agonised lips, 'My

God, Doris, I'll get you for this,' as hasty opinions from poor sports.

Or there was the salt water joke. Ring up all your neighbours in the street in a disguised voice, and tell them you are the local water board and that there has been 'some trouble at the works' and that everyone is to empty 10 lbs of common salt into their fresh water cisterns. Then you ring them all up fifteen minutes later and scream with hilarity.

I'll certainly say this for my folks. What with Mother's intensely funny tricks and Father being always on the point of arriving, or having to leave at once in order to get back in time, we had few lasting friends, but those that passed the test were clearly identifiable as giants of the species.

With a Plummet and Aplomb

I'm a rare bird these days. I do a lot of house calls as they are now called – something of a demand about the very phrase. We used to call it home visiting which sounds much more voluntary, but that was a quarter of a century ago, in England, when as much as half our workload was visiting. I was in Cornwall and perhaps the greatest problem was not the academic side but finding the home of the patient, be it house, cottage, caravan (very common, and mobile, without telling the GP), or farm. Long hours were spent crisscrossing bleak and lonely Bodmin Moor, often at night, with no one to ask the way of. Even if one was lucky enough to find a native for further directions, one was inclined to get Cornish sincerity straight from the elbow. 'Drive ee up ther road quite a way, then take the turn where there's no milk churns left in the hedge anymore.' Mind you, the towns were little better, since they had the odd habit of not putting name plates on the roads, and even residents of many years were ignorant of the name of the street in which they lived. As one explained to me in mild surprise, he knew where he lived so there was no need.

Now in dear old Kiwiland we have different problems and some surprises. Here are two of them.

She was a dear old bean, eighty-five if a day, living alone in her widowhood, and she sent a message for me to call and syringe her ears out. I reckoned it very unlikely that wax alone was the source of her deafness, but all the same my nurse impressed upon her the time and date that I would be beating on her door to have a go, and in due course I rolled up, armed with the necessary equipment, and beat on the door … And beat again. And again. And louder. And harder. And again. Well, there was a total absence of dear old beans letting me in with welcoming smiles to have their ears syringed, so I walked around the house peering in windows until, ah yes, there she was, sitting primly in her little drawing room on a high-backed chair in front of the fire, reading if not the Good Book, then an Improving One. Happily realising my trip had not been thwarted, I tapped politely on the window, gently at first so as not to frighten her. Then harder. Then very vigorously. Then ferociously. I rattled the frame (locked) and began mouthing requests … then impolite suggestions. The stupid old twit, what cretin would lock herself in and then not make a point of expecting me at the arranged time? Idiotic old bag. I bet she's reading *Catch 22* at this very moment, if she's not Joseph Heller himself in disguise.

Well, we deliverers of primary health care in the field and rugged individualists to boot do not give up easily, so I set off around the house again, testing all the doors and windows with the nearest I had to a burglar's jemmy, my plastic tongue spatula. I was rewarded in the end by finding the bathroom window, an old wooden sash affair, distinctly loose. It took time and perseverance but I slowly managed to inch it up until there was a gap large enough to begin to ease myself through. Grabbing my bag I surged upwards and inwards until, with a substantial crash, the window frame gave way, the sill collapsed and I was precipitated not only into the room but into the bath which stood, thankfully empty, under the window. And then the door of the bathroom burst open and the little old lady shot in and hit me on the head with an old chair leg.

On the second occasion, I was visiting a young man of about twenty-five who was 'crook' in bed with something like glandular fever. It is true that I had been sent for, actually by his mother who, like dad, was working so she had said, 'Just go straight in, you know which his room is.' I did, so I did. However, although the young man was undoubtedly unwell, his manner on seeing me was in some indefinable way *distrait*; not really offhand, but the mind preoccupied with perhaps greater thoughts than seeing the doctor when you are ill. I performed my piece, trying to strike a note of cheer into the way I handled my thermometer, and even essaying a little smile when asking him to cough. It all fell on stony ground so I became earnest instead and my advice, particularly when we got to the bit about keeping warm and taking plenty of fluids, was positively intense. Yet still the chord had not been struck, his eyes were blank, and finally I announced that I was going to wash my hands. To my surprise, this rather mundane news produced a definite flicker of emotion across his face. How fascinating it must be to be a psychiatrist and understand the human brain. If I had realised that his interest lay in my ablutions rather than his own health, I would have given him details of how I'd shaved that morning. Silly of me!

Up the hall I went and into the bathroom which sported a hand sink and a bath, the latter shrouded by an opaque plastic curtain. I turned the tap on and reached for the soap. No soap. With piercing intelligence, I thought ha, the last person to use the bath left the soap in the bath, so I brushed back the opaque plastic curtain. There stood the most gorgeous real live and naked blonde.

Funnily enough, in subsequent years we became great friends and have often mused over the utterly superb English aplomb exhibited by myself when I said, 'How do you do, madam. May I trouble you for the soap, please?'

Feast or Famine

I suppose we all have our little megalomanias, if that isn't a contradiction in terms, and I have to be counted. In days gone by, and possibly still, Her Majesty's ships when homeward bound out of the Mediterranean, called at Gibraltar, whereupon the wholesale wine and spirit merchant's rep would come on board and take orders to sustain the ship's company for the long and arduous three days' trip back to the UK. And being very adjacent to Spain, where they invented sherry (named after the town of Jerez, near Cadiz, in case that had slipped your memory), he could always offer a very competitive deal for Tio Pepe or any other of your preference from the bodegas. Most of us would therefore buy gigantic volumes of the stuff; I sometimes wondered if the ship would keel over when the deliveries were made from the wharf, but perhaps the chief engineer jettisoned a couple of thousand gallons of fuel oil to compensate for our alcoholic overload. Anyhow, we never failed to reach home with the precious tincture, and never failed to fail to convince the boarding customs officers in Plymouth Sound that all these bottles, demijohns, vats and forty-four gallon drums were full of vinegar because our wives and mothers were just entering the pickling season. Even as one said the word 'vinegar' in response to the excise man's question you could see him write 'sherry' on the form, but even then the duty was negligible. What it did mean was that once you got your gallons and gallons of the stuff home you had to drink it. Well, I suppose you didn't HAVE to, but there's little point in buying it, even cheap, just to keep, so my wife and I, and our friends, developed the art of drinking sherry often, very often, say three, four, seven times a day, perhaps more when not busy, and come the time my wife wanted one of the demijohns to make into a lamp we had to step up the rate, involve other people such as the postman, and use bigger glasses. In the end the milkman came to expect a pint of sherry every morning and the vicar stopped calling altogether.

Then there was the mother of one of my school friends who, during the war, took on the Ministry of Food's exhortation to preserve food for crises, and began to 'put down', as was the phrase, eggs in a substance called waterglass. You gathered tubs and old baths and the like, filled them with eggs and then topped them up with this clear viscous fluid which, in theory, kept them tolerably like fresh eggs for who knew how long. My mother did a few, and after a bit we took some out and tried them and they were vile. Not rotten, you understand, and they didn't kill us but we all agreed gnawing hunger was infinitely preferable to these disgusting parodies of the erstwhile real thing. But my pal's mother would have none of this; her zeal was unquenchable; she scoured South Devon for more and more containers, entirely filling the cellar, the toolshed and all the spare rooms of her big house with eggs in waterglass. She was still so engaged when the war ended a few years later. I don't know if the council took her house over as a sort of war museum after she died; there was certainly no market for eggs in peacetime which no one would eat in wartime, even if starving.

Slightly more successful was a patient of mine who was made redundant by New Zealand Railways when they converted from steam to diesel and electric engines, for he was an engine driver of steam only and simply couldn't understand electricity. So he tried his hand at market gardening and was miserable in the first year when his cauliflowers failed, pathetic little wizened plants with no flower at all. Well, electricity may have been a closed book but he went to the library and read up cauliflowers. 'It's molybdenum they need, Doc, a trace element and my soil has no molybdenum.' Knowing nothing about it, I took no issue with him, and in due course he scattered molybdenum generously over his patch. Possibly the significance of the description 'trace element' escaped him, or perhaps you can't buy it in minimal amounts, but the results exceeded his wildest dreams. A half acre or so yielded thousands upon thousands upon thousands of cauliflowers, and not one of them was smaller than a bucket and many the size of a twenty-eight-inch TV set. Ours is not a huge town and inevitably he flooded the market so that it was uneconomic to harvest them. He kindly gave me a lot, such that for many weeks we had a mound of slowly rotting cauliflowers behind the garage, and ate only cabbage for the rest of the winter.

Behind the garage in the garden of an elderly patient of mine appeared an ocean-going yacht, costing

$750,000 which, in those days, was a GREAT deal of money. My eighty-seven-year-old pensioner had won over two million on Lotto.

'I always wanted a yacht, Doctor, and now I can afford one,'

'What are you going to do with it?' I asked.

'Nothing. I can't sail and even if I could I'm too old for that sort of thing. It's a pity really. But it's a very nice yacht.' I went home and had a cold shower.

There is a shower in a bed and breakfast establishment where we once spent the night which is at the head of the stairs, four floors up. The odd thing is that it is free standing, yes, a shower cabinet in the middle of the landing. Its walls are frosted glass but all the same you can see, when it is in use, a pink body oodling about inside, soaping and rinsing and washing its hair. Where its clothes are I know not, nor how it determines the moment to exit and make a quick dash for room 23A or wherever, but I told my wife I would be going to bed that night sweaty and dirty, not negotiable.

This on one of our tours of England, while at another – why did we always seem to get the top floor – the plumbing of the toilet was charged by a system described on a label on the cistern as "Patent Pressure Power Rocket". I used the machine in the natural way without concern, and minutes later my spouse took her turn. She returned to our room somewhat flustered.

'It won't stop. I stopped but it didn't. It's nearly at the top already.'

So, being the gentleman, I essayed a recce. Certainly the tide was surging, so I pulled the handle again. The menace increased and before my very eyes the Patent Pressure Power Rocket erupted with muted roar and the contents cascaded over the rim. I fled. We phoned the desk.

'It can't do that. The system doesn't work like that.'
I looked out of our doorway.

'Yes it can.'

'Someone will come up and see.'

'They'll be too late soon, it's coming down to see you.'

And as I spoke the Patent Pressure Power Rocket patently pressed its produce under the door of the loo, across the landing and down the stairs to the next landing. And the one below. And it was still pressure powering as we packed our bags and sought the fire escape to avoid the Niagara on the main stairs.

Heads You Win, Tails I Lose

When I asked Miss Hall how she spent rainy days when she couldn't garden, she replied that she baked for the elderly in the parish. Miss Hall is ninety-one.

And old Miss Lewis rang me up for an urgent house visit.

'It's my brother Hubert, he's had an accident with the car and he's very muddly, must have hit his head or something,'

'Where is he now?' I asked.

'Oh, he's at home now.'

Knowing how difficult it was to turn a car at the top of their drive, I left mine at the gate and walked up the garden path to the back door. Elsie let me in.

'He's in the dining room, Doctor.'

And so he was. He was not only in the dining room but he was also still in his car. Which was also in the dining room. And in the wall of the dining room, where it faced onto the top of the drive which I had eschewed, was a large hole in the brickwork which exactly matched the silhouette of Hubert's Morris Minor.

'I was backing too fast so I pressed hard on the brake pedal, Doctor. But it was the accelerator.'

Which reminds me not of a patient but a colleague in arms when I and a dozen other conscript doctors were doing our introductory course in the Royal Navy, the theme of which was that we should experience as far as possible situations which our service patients may have suffered and need our treatment for. Most of this I found extremely unpleasant, such as having your arms blown up by a simulated but nevertheless very painful depth charge, or shot up a ramp by an explosive charge the same as that which expels pilots from their crashing aircraft. To find Hubert so unexpectedly in his car at home reminded me of the day we had to don diving suits and plunge around in a massive water tank, watched by our instructors through portholes in the tank, they being comfortable and dry outside the portholes. Being a victim of claustrophobia, I elected a free swim frogman format since I shuddered at the thought of the old-fashioned leather/rubber suit with huge steel helmet and gigantic boots, each weighted with 7 lb lead soles. But not Eric, not he. It took them hours to insert him into it, screw his head on, or, rather, his helmet, it made little difference, and encase his feet in the leaden boots. We'd done our stuff by then, so we trooped down to watch Eric through the portholes. The water was not clear, indeed it was very murky to the point of being almost opaque, and for a while we saw no sign of our intrepid friend. Then, however, a deeper darkness began to manifest itself at one side and began to take on a vague outline.

'Here he comes.' He drifted, very slowly, closer, still much of a blur. Now closer and we began to mutter. Now close, and we stared with awe. He was upside down. Slowly, slowly Eric drifted past our numbed

gaze, his pale face discernibly giving us a weak smile as
it began to merge into the haze again. Fourteen pounds
of lead on his feet and he was upside down …

The instructors looked upset and hurried away to
retrieve Eric, who ultimately seemed none the worse
for wear though a trifle taciturn and we wondered if
he had been taken through a special reading of the
Official Secrets Act.

I suppose Eric survived the course; we went separate
ways after a while and I never saw an obituary to
him, although it did surprise me considering our next
induction. This entailed being dressed in a pilot's
flying gear, with parachute harness and one man
rubber dinghy strapped on your back, and then being
suspended just under the roof of Portsmouth municipal
swimming pool. When it came to my turn, I remember
thinking that the pool looked so small from that
height that I wondered if I would miss it altogether
when they let me fall. Which, you see, was the drill.
One moment you were dangling, the next you were
flying through the air, downwards (which is, perhaps,
not strictly speaking, flying) until you hit the water,
whereupon you performed a series of actions which
released your parachute and inflated your dinghy, into
which you gratefully climbed. Then came the nasty
bit; an instructor swam up to you, turned you and
the dinghy upside down and encouraged you to find
a way of righting the bloody thing and getting back
into it. As luck would have it, my procedures all went
according to plan. Despite my doubts, I hit the pool,
not the concrete verges, and all else went well, even
getting back into my vessel despite my instructor, and
at this stage I was left to bob and watch my colleagues
try their luck. Most also succeeded until, of course,
we came to Eric, who had reached the stage of being

capsized by his official. After which nothing much happened. His dinghy bobbed for a bit, it twitched in an unnatural way, it lay silent in the water, it twitched a bit more. At no stage did it look remotely as if it was going to come right way up again, bearing Eric in its bosom. After a bit his instructor lifted the edge of the dinghy to see if all was well. One saw Eric's face hanging down from it (we began to wonder if we would ever recognise Eric if we met him in the street, right way up) and again we were treated to an enigmatic, if wistful, smile.

'Try a bit harder, sir,' he was told, and he disappeared underwater again as the instructor let go.

Much the same performance occurred, with no success, and the next time the dinghy was elevated Eric's face (upside down OF COURSE) was rather bluish, and his smile, though still enigmatic, was much more wistful. They fished him out and he recovered. I believe.

Yet another trial for young naval doctors was to be set down in the middle of the night in the middle of the New Forest, in a group, and told to find our way back to Portsmouth barracks within forty-eight hours without using any money nor hitchhiking. It was an initiative test and we won hands down. No money meant no cash, as Nelson would have understood it, but one of our number had a credit card, one of the first possibly in England at that time, which enabled us, with means with which I shall not bore you, to hire two taxis and be back in Barracks for breakfast of the same day. We expected to be promoted to captain to a man, or at least get the V.C., but Their Lordships inexplicably took a dim view of success and shortly after we were dispersed to ships and shore stations various, in all parts of the globe, unpromoted and with no V.C.s.

The Waiting Game

I don't know how you feel about meeting people at airports, but I seem to have the most phenomenal bad luck. It's hard enough meeting people I know but when, for example, I have to meet a locum with whom I've only corresponded, the problem is obvious.

I have asked other people how they circumvent this, only to get airy replies that one just says 'Gidday' to the first likely looking mortal and that's it. But it is not it, not when I do that.

I once said, 'Gidday', to so many people getting off a plane that a nearby policeman began to eye me in an unmistakeable and significant way, and those travellers whom I had accosted who didn't share the copper's nasty inferences began to gather around me in an ever-swelling mob, under the impression that I was their tour guide.

Promising subjects

It is just as bad to peer closely at promising looking

subjects. Some ignore you, others shy away, and a few wink. The totally polite approach, 'Excuse me, I'm so sorry to bother you, but I am seeking a Dr Alfred Gortonthwaide-Bolster, are you he?', is very exhausting when applied to upwards of two hundred males, and, despite the courtesy, gets some pretty vulgar replies.

Then there is paging. I have, when on holiday and in pubs where you buy a meal and they sing out your number when it is cooked, been asked to use my rich baritone (something to do with my Welsh ancestry) to bellow out numbers over the hubbub of the cheery crowd, and in such mellow circumstances I have been happy to oblige, but I'm dashed if I'm going to wade around my hometown airport lounge, exposed to many of my customers, shouting names like a bingo caller. Nor can I bring myself to stand and shout my own name every fifteen seconds, in case they think I've gone loopy, or the opposition feel I'm advertising.

No, well then, I tried another dodge. I forewarned the locum that I would stand in an area well apart from where the greeting friends and relatives usually stand, and that I would stare fixedly at the clock suspended as it is from a nearby balcony.

This I did on the day in question, but on that particular day fate would have it that a large cadre of colleagues turned up to wait and welcome an equally large body of overseas colleagues – I thought for one moment that the hospital must have burned down quickly and we were setting up emergency services here, until I remembered that it was the eve of a major professional conference in our town. Well, all chums and buddies, they swarmed around me, chatting of this and that, and try as I may to stand separately and be seen looking at the clock, I remained in the centre of a crowd, and, being short, totally obscured to would-be locums.

The only success I have achieved has been the umbrella technique, and that is qualified. Our part of Godzone has a sparse rainfall, and it is rarely that one needs a brolly, so here my ruse was to carry a very large black one as ostensibly as possible, in fact wave it around like Nureyev rehearsing for the finale.

Looking different

You see, it is quite impossible to dress in unusual clothes anymore, since the present generation live in unusual clothes, in my opinion, as a matter of custom. If one was to wait attired in pink pyjama trousers, riding boots with spurs, a bare torso and 'Charlie' painted on a half-shaven scalp in green lipstick, one would probably find one was only seventh in a row of similar nightmares.

But the black brolly gets them nearly every time, I should say an eighty per cent success rate, the failures being due to unhappy days when it actually does rain and there are eleven of us so armed. Of course, you have to put up with some stares because an umbrella does not go with white shirt, shorts and walk socks, but that is the whole idea (and yet they don't stare at the green painted Charlies?) …

The next item is the unbelievable difficulties I have meeting people I already know. At Christmas my wife and I went to meet our two daughters returning from the UK for the holidays. Our local airport is a quiet, comfortable little place. The flight controllers have a busy morning rush when three planes within half an hour take off for the other centres, and then there is a lull until lunchtime when the hang-gliders practice, and after that the sheep are put on the field until the three morning planes come back for tea.

Well, that's how it used to be, and I had forgotten that we now have a rival airline, and the unbelievable happened and two planes arrived within half a minute of each other. Naturally, we met the wrong one, and having seen all its passengers disembark, and turned away in mortal disappointment, we found our girls standing behind us, equally disappointed at not being met.

Unavoidably detained

On another occasion we were meeting old friends, but unavoidably arrived late; one drives past the airport doors to get to the car park, and as we were doing just that, we realised that our friends were just emerging through the doors. In the way the traffic is channelled, I was unable to stop, so I elected to drive straight through the car park, out, and come round again, collecting our pals at the second swoop.

But to get out of the car park you have to feed a certain coin to that silly arm thing to make it swing up, and I couldn't find the right coin. By the time I did, our friends, who had seen us drive past them to begin with, had followed us into the car park, toting their heavy luggage and cursing us somewhat, only to see the arm thing elevate, as I had found the right money, and us drive away from them once again.

Of course, I didn't know this, and drove around to the door again as nippily as I could, only to find them not there, so again I entered the car park, this time just as they were coming back out of it, and would have run straight over them if they hadn't abandoned their cases and leaped into the bushes on the verge as

I swept past again. They never forgot this, and when they visit us now they take care to arrive in the city unannounced. They say hitchhiking is preferable to being met by us.

Then there was the occasion I went to meet an old friend whom I hadn't seen since student days, and we both found each other so hard to recognise that we stood around until the concourse was empty and the cleaners moved in at the end of the day, by which time we both reasoned that the other wizened, aged, dissolute, ravaged, shrivelled old crone must be jolly old Botters from days very much of yore … Good Lord, I'm glad I don't look as terrible as that, I wonder why he didn't recognise me.

Idle amusement

And I haven't been there for several years now, but the arrival mechanism at Sydney really takes the cake if you want a bit of idle amusement. For those who haven't tried it, it is the opposite of, say, Heathrow, where, once you have been through all the customs and immigration and etc., you enter a long long long passageway with a concrete wall on one side, and a rail on the other. Behind this the entire population of London stand, in one long phalanx stretching to the horizon, as does the passage.

If you haven't seen someone you know by the time you have walked to the end of the passage, you are the greatest nobody on earth. (In fact, I have found it rather embarrassing because there really are so many friends and relatives to pick from that I have several times approached those who I thought were mine, with a winsome smile and open arms, only to find on drawing near that they are quite like my kin but not actually them. So one draws away, feeling a bit silly and tries again further down the passage.)

But Sydney does it differently. After the customs and etc., etc., you approach a small door in a wall. Upon opening same, and passing through it, you find yourself on a stage, all alone, and looking down on an immense sea of faces, the entire population of Sydney, no doubt.

There is no walking past, sampling the goods. You just stand there, and if you weren't ready for it, you gape. I've never been met there by anyone, so I don't delay in jumping down from the stage and heading off through the milling mob, but to anyone who has to scan some two million faces for Auntie, it must be a long task.

I confess an impish whim prompted me to wave on one occasion, and to my delight, 806 people in various parts of the hall waved back. I was so sorely tempted to do a short tap dance, or perhaps even start to undress, slowly, whistling a bump and grind tune as I went, but I'm glad I didn't because I told one of my daughters about it later and next time she went through Sydney she was able to be the first person to do it ...

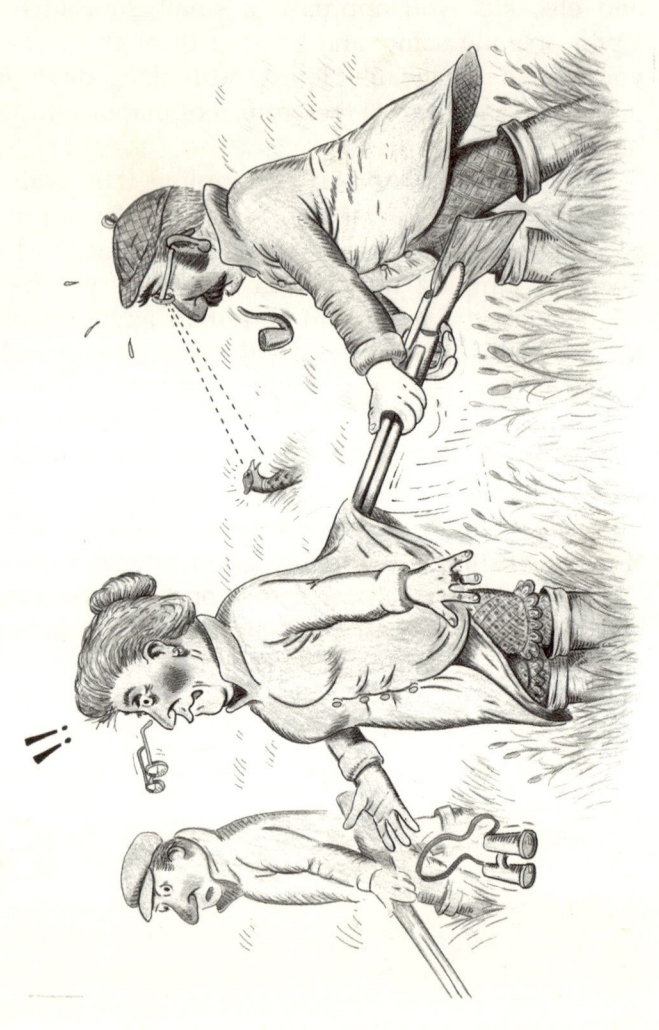

Talking Turkey

I was in the Post Office the other day, queuing as usual because although there are four serving hatches it is policy that only two at most, and often only one, is manned. Well, as I stood there, my eye was caught by a poster on the wall which announced that the largest turkey farm in the world was in Norfolk, that it contained 7,900,000 turkeys, and that 2,300 people were required to look after these birds. I am glad to know this, and that some of the enormous postage which I spend weekly is devoted to researching matters to enrich my life. Or possibly the Postmaster General has a matchbox collection from which he is able to withdraw these choice revelations free of charge to us, the public financers.

But it brought to mind that it is now the duck shooting season, at least as I write this, if not when you read it, and I wondered if his matchboxes can tell us how many million ducks there are flying around and how many people banging away at them. I think I've mentioned in these columns before that I'm not a camping, roughing it man. I prefer to see the ducks on my plate, anointed with orange sauce, cradled in green peas and all ready to jump onto my fork.

But let it not be said that I don't give things a go. It was in Norfolk that I was introduced to duck shooting – had I known then that there were over seven million turkeys lurking about over the paddocks offering a soft touch, I'd have gone for them, but alas, the English post offices are not so erudite as ours.

My stepfather, a gaunt, taciturn to the point of acid, retired bank manager was my guide and mentor, a very keen and experienced 'gun'. We left his home in Stamford and drove east, out of Lincs and into Norfolk, for what seemed like days. Then we left the car, shouldered guns, ammo, bags, groundsheets, bags, clothes extra, boxes, food and drink and bags, and walked east for what seemed like days. We must, he said, in one burst of volubility, reach the right spot. After a bit, we had to crawl and wade with guns, ammo, bags, ground-sheets, etc. The essence, he contributed, another hour later as we struggled on, was to be concealed *in situ* at a certain pond over which the ducks would come in from the sea in the evening gloom. Which is what it then was, even putting it charitably. However, the anticipation of the thrills of the barrage and the huge succulent meals to come overcame my increasing dislike of the Iron Man training we were going through.

Well, in due course the ducks came in, as predicted. Both of them. At 37,000 feet, just below a Stockholm–New York jumbo. Being abysmally ignorant of guns and these things, I at first thought that my relation's disinclination to pull the trigger was in case he hit the jumbo, and I hoped the birds hadn't learned to time their flights with those of the European flight timetables. But such was not the case. Apparently the bullets won't get that high, even if you swing the barrel up with a jaunty twirl at the moment of firing, as I have seen done. No, the relative sucked on his empty pipe in a querulous way, and to my horror, began to pack up the equipment. I gathered that if those two heralds of the quacking population were flying that high, so would the rest, and that was our day.

That was, as it turned out, my entire life at duck shooting, and my diffidence was so obvious that the old chap said that pheasant shooting was *completely* different when he asked me to accompany him on the local shoot, a rather snobby affair with much social and sporting etiquette to be rigorously observed. My mother loves a bit of chat with 'country people', being a snob herself, so she came along too. Horace, my stepfather, brought his latest gun dog, an exuberant young spaniel which he wished to train, and off we went.

This time it was only a couple of miles from home, and all relatively civilised. You put on warm clothes and big boots, and you simply walked across an enormous field of kale, a sort of rough cabbage on long stalks. There were about thirty of us, spaced out at five yard intervals, acting as our own beaters so that the pheasants would rise in front of us and we would let fly, and then the dogs pick up the fallen, and what could be simpler?

But it was not to be. Mother is a sociable chatty type and this walking five yards apart was not to her liking and she kept closing in, gradually but repeatedly, so that she didn't have to shout to her neighbours all the vital information about her new hat or something. 'Spread out, Doris, spread out,' was the oft-repeated injunction from her husband, but to no lasting avail.

She was alongside him again when the pheasant rose slightly to one side, and my stepfather's shot gun automatically and reflexively swung around and up. It went up inside my mother's heavy tweed coat, and some say that from the tone with which she screamed 'HorACE', it went up inside her skirt too. What fabulous control prevented Horace from pulling one if not both triggers will never be known, but Mother survives to this day. Then the eager spaniel rushed off, terrified by the scream, but re-emerged from the kale later with a live, un-shot pheasant in its mouth, a monumental no-no in the shooting community of the Midland counties that guarantees ostracism for life.

As I said, Horace was not a loquacious man. He used a few words derived from the trenches in the First World War, and has not spoken since.

Break a Leg

My patient had a broken leg. I reduced the fracture (i.e. set the bones, for lay readers) and immobilised it in plaster. My first, my very first. I was a young casualty officer, doing a twelve-month stint in a busy Accident and Emergency department of a large hospital in a city in southern England, population a quarter of a million, plus another quarter of a million rustics outside the city limits.

There were two of us juniors plus the Boss on during the day, and a third junior on at night, on a roster basis. There were always lots of broken bones coming in, especially during the winter, and this was my debut night solo. I ensconced my patient in a cubicle for the rest of the night, and in the morning the Boss would review him, as per routine, to ensure that we'd done the right thing.

Everyone called the Boss "Daddy"; he was paternal, kind, very experienced and a peerless physician and surgeon, and he was full of knowledge and wisdom (some academics would be surprised to know that these are not the same thing).

Bursting with pride, I presented my broken leg. Two of the patient's relatives were present, together with the theatre sister and two junior nurses. I couldn't resist a furtive glance at the audience perchance to witness their undoubted adulation and admiration of my expert prowess. Actually, their faces were rather blank, but I took that to be awe in the presence of genius. And now, the master himself.

As was his wont, an impassive face, a grave manner, he inspected my handiwork in silence. He then said:

'Williams ...' (and I hoped the patient and his relatives would remember that, in case I went into private practice) '... Williams, that is the worst plaster I have ever seen in my entire life.' He needed a little more breath. 'If we leave it on and this man is lucky, he will lose his leg; if he is unlucky he will lose his life ... Take it off, cut it off, and I will then show you how it should be done.'

His words scalded my ears and I thought they would melt and run off my head. Then I offered a deal with Fate; if the floor would open up and swallow me, I wouldn't try to get back up again; but Fate wasn't negotiating, and I spent the next half hour hacking off my lumpy abomination, after which Daddy encased the leg in a superlative work of professional and aesthetic art. Slim, straight, slender yet strong, the foot pointing the right way and at the right angle, the finish smooth, yea glossy, it shone with elegance and functional perfection. The theatre sister, of vast experience, nodded with tacit pleasure, the relatives and junior nurses beamed their approbation and naked hero-worship, and the patient, now free of pain, un-creased his face to one of relief. I hoped he'd forgotten my name, in case I went into private practice. In any case, I had resolved to lock myself in the toilet at elevenses and drink a gallon of hemlock.

But when Daddy had finished, and I perceived what he had done, a strange thing came over me; it was something more than a very steep, short learning curve.

For the next few weeks he inspected my plasters of the night, impassive as usual, but ending with a nod and 'Good'. After that he didn't inspect them at all. You see, he was a wise man. He not only treated that man very well but he ensured that the many, many patients who would come under my care in the future would also be treated very well.

He could have said to me, 'That's not too bad a plaster but we'll adjust it a bit, shall we?' Or: 'OK for starters but I'll just add a wee refinement or two.' Or: 'Under the circumstances, I understand; a slight alteration, perhaps?' Or, he could have taken me aside and said, in private, what he had said to me in front of an audience, loudly and clearly.

Any of these alternatives would have resulted in better plasters by Williams, better but not the best, some even possibly indifferent. What he did resulted in the BEST. They were not, they never could be, on a par with Daddy's, but instead of drinking hemlock, I caused the theatre sister to nod approval, the relatives, and even the patients, to smile with relief.

What Daddy did was to mean that, in times to come, young doctors came to me and asked me to show them 'how it should be done'.

I showed them, not with conceit, but happy and humble that Daddy had known what to teach me and, wisely, how to teach me.

On behalf of a truly enormous number of people, Daddy, I salute you.

As Easy As Winking?

I have one long-sighted eye and one short-sighted eye; remember that, because it's germane to my story. I am also a man of habit, and for the past twenty years or more it has been my custom to always have my haircut, buy a Kiwi ticket and pick up the newspaper at a little alcove of a shop which nestles in the foyer of one of the larger hotels in our fair city.

And this is just what I did last week. As I stepped out into the sunshine again, pocketing the ticket, folding the paper and patting my shortened coiffure, I chanced to glance up towards the windows of a block of offices across the road, and there, standing in one of the windows, was a remarkably beautiful young lady.

Well, I'm not quite so old yet that I can't appreciate such visions, but to get full value at that range it is necessary to close the short-sighted eye so that my brain can go all out for the clear image in the long-sighted one. So this is what I did and I saw that she was indeed a very lovely person. Rather to my surprise, she waved at me. Reflexively, I opened both eyes wide, but then closed the short-sighted one again to see if, in fact, she was someone I knew. She wasn't, but she waved again. I then realised that what I was doing must, to the uninitiated, look as if I was winking!

Now embarrassed, I walked on, but nonetheless I felt secretly pretty chuffed because not even in the heyday of my youth could I pull the girls in with one wink at thirty yards. Perhaps it was the haircut? Should I go back and tell old Bob that he had really got the secret with the scissors? I decided against it, but jokingly to myself I thought I would put it to the test again, for there, at about the sixth floor of the same office block I espied another female form looking roughly in my direction. Shut the starboard eye, full ahead with the port and yes, bless my soul, the result was electric. She waved with a gusto which left her predecessor far behind. It was quite remarkable. I smiled, trying not to look condescending, and also twitched my newspaper because I was still slightly embarrassed. I mean, it's one thing to discover that you have a magnetic charm, but in all modesty I'm not sure that I can handle it now. What a pity I hadn't had that haircut or that pseudo-wink thirty years ago, when, I found, it took me all evening, and several more usually, to persuade young ladies that I was a real catch. Now, like learning to swim or ride a bicycle, I found I had the knack. But then also, I didn't want to appear as if I was set on picking up every dame in town. Dash it, what would the wife say?

In the interests of science and research, however, I thought I'd try it just once more, and really make it tough for myself. This time up to the eleventh floor, where luckily another subject awaited my left eyeball. It was quite astonishing. I admit that this time it did take two 'winks', but allowing for the fact that the lady herself must be assumed to have incredible visual acuity to even see my expression (let alone whether I had one eye shut or not) at that distance, I felt I could still reasonably claim a 100 per cent record so far. Actually it became a 130 per cent record – she must have communicated to her office because she was joined by another lass who began waving before I had the chance to function. This time I waved back, newspaper in fist, a full-blooded response. Obviously I was in demand, and I must give something back to my public. I walked on, well pleased, humming a gentle melody and pondering on what a lucky person my wife was.

The clock on the brewery showed 10.45 a.m. which reminded me that the cricket – England versus our chaps – playing here in fact, started at 11 a.m. I wouldn't be able to go and watch though, as I was due in surgery for the rest of the day. But there was a man leaning over the parapet of the brewery roof, and to my horror, when I glanced at the clock, he waved and I hadn't winked, indeed. I lowered my gaze at once and walked on. Two secretaries in another office block, next to the brewery both waved and one blew kisses. I had not deliberately 'winked' at them – or was I doing it without even knowing? Was it getting out of control? Or was my charisma flowing out of me to swamp the entire population with affection for Yours Truly? Perhaps I had been knighted and they had forgotten to tell me, but put my picture in the paper anyhow. For services to gardening, was all I could think of. It seemed a bit thin but surely even the most superb haircut could scarcely engender all this adulation. Three oldish ladies in another window waved (of course) and I was relieved to note that a man with them merely stared at me.

Well, in for a penny, in for a pound, and for the remainder of my stroll to the car park I rather enjoyed myself, responding with gracious waves closely modelled on Her Majesty's style, with clean smiles and tasteful tilting of the head. Upon reaching my car, I dropped my keys and as I straightened from picking them up, I came face to face with Mike Gatting, the captain of the English cricket team, and tall blond beautiful Graham Dilley, and ditto Jarvis, and Athey, and Emburey, and eight young virile debonair Englishmen, all in immaculate whites, some carrying bats. They were walking from their hotel (the one with a little alcove of a barber's shop in the foyer which sells papers and Kiwi tickets) to the fleet of cars waiting in the car park to take them to the ground.

Ours Not to Reason Why

The colleague was an American gentleman, from the Mid West actually, and the title of his lecture was: 'The Genetics of Sucrose Metabolism in *Streptococcus Mutans*'. I didn't go because I thought it might cover ground with which I was already familiar ... and I didn't think I would understand it either.

However, I did marvel that anyone, *anyone*, would know enough about what must surely be a limited subject to be able to fluff it out into an hour-long lecture, and I suppose it just goes to show that, indeed, specialists know a great deal about very little. But I have to blow the gaff on this erudite scholar's fellow countrymen; they don't all know what makes *s. mutans* tick, neither do they know where Canada is.

My elder son just so happens to be living in the Mid West, albeit a trifle further north than our lecturer, and he is a truthful young man (my son, not the lecturer – well I mean I expect the lecturer is truthful too, but I can only vouch for my son). Where was I? Yes, I can promise you that there are some sons of A Lincoln who do not know where Canada is ...

And I can add to that, again courtesy of my kin across the Pacific. One day he was delighted to espy kiwifruit for sale in the local store, and swarmed in to buy some. On the counter there was more promotion: 'Delicious Kiwifruit, all the way from Sunny ... (wait for it) ... California!' Well naturally my lad took them to task in some measure, pointing out that the place for kiwifruit to come from was Kiwiland, viz New Zealand. To this came the reply, 'So what, Noo Zealand's part of Arstralia, ain't it?'

Well those of us who have been abroad, i.e. beyond the Chathams, will sadly be used to the upsetting misconception that we're Aussies. Indeed, I have educated friends in London who are quite sure that we can see Sydney across 'the straight', rather like you can see Boulogne across the English Channel from Dover.

So my son wearily set about enlightening the shopkeeper. However, being a bright, as well as honest, lad, he went on to point out that even if we were part of 'Arstralia', what was the thrust of the American argument, to which that worthy replied, 'Well, Arstralia's part of the States, same as California, ain't it, so why the beef?' And his mate down the road lectures on sucrose metabolism, and in *streptococcus mutans*, to boot.

The magic screen

Quite apart from which, let me tell you about the old folks' rest home which I visited recently in order to see one of my elderly patients temporarily in residence. Being familiar with the ground plan, I peeked in her room to see if she was there, but she wasn't, so I headed for the communal lounge where I guessed she would be, with her cronies.

I was correct; there they all were, sitting in a carefully arranged semicircle of which the focus was the television table sited in the corner of the room, and from which some jolly music and repartee was emanating. I confess that, had a test match been on, I just might have paused in my errand of mercy and healing long enough to watch for a couple of hours or more, depending on the play and the pitch.

But my ears told me instantly that such was not the case and I made a beeline for Florrie in the centre of the semicircle, to give of my wisdom and generally zap her up a bit. She seemed to be the better for this, even to the extent towards the end of our tête-a-tête of asking who I was. I encouraged her not to worry and she said, 'What about?', so I felt that therapy was over for the day, and anyhow, wasn't that the theme music from a James Bond movie starting on the box?

Perhaps I would just have a peak before I left at the magic screen, so I turned to look. I went on turning. I turned back. Florrie was watching. I turned to those on her right. They were watching. I turned to those on her left. They were watching too. Engrossed they were. Fascinated would be another *mot just*. I turned back to the TV table.

The king with no clothes. There was nothing on the table. Nothing at all. Zilch, to use the term from the man from the Mid West (storekeeper or lecturer, take your pick). The table was bare. It was, it is true, arranged exactly where they could all see it, without having to crane, without having to jostle each other and argue. But there was still nothing on it. There was a small loudspeaker lying on the floor behind, and the unmistakeable crescendos of 'Goldfinger' were coming from it, but of spectacle there was none. So I bid my farewell, and was careful to sidle out of the room in such a way that I didn't get between the viewers and the table.

No end to it

There was no end to it that day. Another geriatric visit, to a dear old bean who had been into clinics various to tend her stomach and her hearing and her cataracts and her arthritis. The last lot had given her a felt collar for her creaking neck, but when I called I found her wearing the collar around the lower half of her face, looking something like a deep sea diver with his helmet removed. You could just see her eyes and forehead above it, and her voice came out in a muffled blur. She said she found it difficult to eat because, to get food into her mouth, she had to lift the collar up … and then she couldn't see. I told her it was meant to go around her neck, to which she replied that I was as silly as the hospital doctor, because how could she do it up around her neck when her arthritis prevented her getting her arms up to her neck. No, she said, it was better where it was; at least it kept her nose warm.

Then there was the chap who went for an exercise ECG. 'How did you get on?' I asked him.

'I got an angina pain before I even got on the bicycle thing.'

'You mean without any exercise at all? Good heavens, were you worried about something?'

'Not until I got there. Then they opened a box thing and turned a switch on. "Just warm this up first," they said. It was marked on the side "Defibrillator". That's when I got the pain.'

Striking a Sympathetic Nerve

'This,' he said, 'is going to be a big job.' A great wave of weakness pervaded the bowels, and my knees felt like jelly. 'I'll do the best I can,' he went on, 'but it can never be the same as the original. You see, it's really a complete rebuild job. If we make a start on Monday we might be finished by the end of the week.'

Two separate men said the above to me last week, almost exactly word-for-word, and my reaction in each case was the same. The first was my garage man, surveying the bent metal which had been my car until a lady aimed her car at it while it stood harmlessly in the road outside the house of the patient I was visiting – and scored a bullseye. The second was my dentist, a stranger whom I avoid like the plague but whose company I was forced to seek after an interval of nine and a half years because I broke a tooth laughing so hard at a story Henry Blofeld told while waiting for the rain to stop in a cricket commentary.

'Actually,' the ogre said, 'you have broken two teeth,' and then he led into the gloomy monologue above, just as if he had been having coaching by my garage man.

Well, the big jobs are over. The car wasn't so bad because the lady came clean and offered to pay, and the only real upset was having to rely upon my wife and my nurse to kindly chauffeur me around for a few days, a circumstance calculated to engender among my less charitable public the notion that I had lost my licence, not my car.

On the other hand the dental experience was an ordeal, as I knew it would be. I am the only man I know to have a local anaesthetic even for an inspection. To get that in they have to turn up the piped music to VERY LOUD and ask the Fire Department to practise sounding the alarm. When my screams have died down they let the other patients back into the waiting room. Five times I went and five times this terrible business went on and five times I had to recover. The latter stage is a major torture. Although it is true that my wife and nurse (two separate people, I should add) expressed some muted sympathy, it was clear that they had no comprehension of the suffering I was so bravely enduring. As I was forced to patiently explain, for it was not by any means for the first time, even if I could not feel the pain the thought that I might do so was virtually as excruciating. And anyhow I was, *per se* and *ipso facto*, a patient for once and, *ipso facto* again, in the category of being sympathised with and generally cosseted, not to say treated well. I am sorry to record that their memories were short and there were several instances when I was compelled to limp in order to tacitly remind them that I was ill – a really disgraceful state of affairs.

Then there was the matter of the local anaesthetic itself, apart from its injection referred to already. On the penultimate occasion an inferior dental block was called for. I think my man managed to impale the left side of my spinal cord as well because not only did my jaw go numb, but my left ear also, so that when I was putting my stethoscope in my ears a few hours later I missed altogether on that side, giving the impression that it had fallen off. Mind you, I have given inferior dentals myself when doing my time in Her Majesty's forces at sea. It was a small vessel like a frigate where it was the duty of the ship's doctor to be the dentist as well. Many are the merry tales I could tell about being on the giving end; filling, filing, pushing and pulling, with the aid of a paper-backed handbook issued by the Admiralty to amateur dentists. But, the occasion I have most in mind was when I thought I was giving but found I was receiving. I think the instructions were something about inserting your index finger in the patient's mouth, passing it along the ramus of the mandible as far as the last molar and then inserting your loaded syringe and needle along the line of your finger to its full extent whereupon, bingo, the tip of the needle would be adjacent to the inferior dental nerve and you gave your all in a good squirt. My squirt was anticipated by milliseconds by the ship giving a good roll and I neatly anaesthetised my own finger. Funnily enough I thought then that my intending patient would have given me some sympathy, but instead he leapt out of the chair and was gone, his toothache apparently miraculously cured.

Well, there you are, patients do some most peculiar things – they're just not like other human beings. Take the case of the newspaper wetter for example. This is a middle-aged lady with very advanced emphysema and asthma who is now so incapacitated that she cannot leave her home and just sits around swallowing pills, inhaling inhalants, breathing oxygen fresh from the cylinder through those plastic tube 'spectacles' into her nose, and doing crosswords. It is my custom to visit her at home, usually calling on a Monday when I am in her locality.

On this particular occasion, Monday had been filled out with crises and I had to postpone my call until Wednesday, in fact, so she was not expecting me. Not that this mattered because I always let myself in via the back door into the kitchen, which is what I now did. She was sitting at the kitchen table with all her paraphernalia, wheezing and blowing gently and reading the morning paper. 'Hallo, Mrs G, just me again. Better late than never,' I breezed. Rather to my astonishment, her eyes appeared above the top of the paper in an unmistakable expression of total horror. I realise that I am not everyone's idea of a pretty face but I was even less prepared for her next action. She rose from her chair (plastic 'spectacles' and all) and conveyed the newspaper to the sink where, to my now bursting amazement, she turned on both taps and plunged the paper under them, wetting it thoroughly and mulching and kneading it as if it was tomorrow's bread. Seeming satisfied with the pulpy mass produced in such short order, she turned the taps off and left it to soak as naturally as if it was the week's laundry. She resumed her seat, whereupon we indulged in a banal conversation which totally ignored the pantomime I had just witnessed. Which just goes to show that, whatever the psychologists say, human behaviour does not always follow a pattern.

To prove that I am not just a pretty face (to some people) I have made a point, ever since this episode, of telephoning the lady first to say I'm on my way because I have no wish to share with her in future the risk of being blown sky high as the oxygen ignites from the cigarette she says she doesn't smoke as she reads the daily.

A Chapter of Accidents?

The good lady and I recently spent some weeks visiting our sons and daughters in England, and nephews and nieces and sundry others, all of whom seemed pleased to see us and delighted that we weren't staying.

We have some friends who live in Windsor (yes, actually next door to the York place, ho ho) who had mistaken the dates and were just off for a weekend in the south of France when we arrived at their place. They gamely unpacked and broke out the champagne, but were terribly miffed later in our tour when we failed to turn up on the weekend when they thought we would. I had already explained that we were, that weekend, visiting my sister and her family in Devon, where a general family picnic was to be held on Budleigh Salterton beach.

It was, as usual in summer in England, blowing a force seven with a rising sea and a thin icy rain, but we Anglo-Saxons care nothing for such trifling inconveniences, and, in our honour, the family congregated on the grey damp beach and huddled under rain capes eating the revolting English sausage roll and inhaling beer from tins.

Deficient mouth

I say inhaling with accuracy, in my case. Perhaps I have a deficient mouth or my lips are not rosebud-like, but I have never been able to develop the facility that the entire younger generation seems to be born with and that is of fitting their mouths to the inconveniently oval hole in drink tins. It is set too far from the edge of the tin to be able to sip, and it is further compromised by the ring attachment which tears it open.

I hope the manufacturers are paying due attention, though I suppose it matters little to them whether my lager trickles down my chin or gets breathed in. In fact, I expect they prefer it that way because the customer has to buy three tins to be able to ingest the equivalent of one.

Where was I? Ah yes, well all was going along in this jolly fashion, when we showed my niece's younger son how to set the sails on his prize possession, a model yacht just received for his birthday. It went along at an amazing speed on a starboard tack, but with this setting, in the brisk gale prevailing, it left the beach and cleared the headland and, presumably, has by now reached Brazil, since there is no intervening land on the course it had adopted. We tried to comfort the heartbroken youth by telling him we would look out for it on Dunedin beach and post it back ...

Not content

Not content with ruining his life, and offending the neighbours of the Duke of York (got it in again), we went on to farewell our younger son who was leaving soon after the Budleigh beach party to resume his tour of European centres of antiquity and beer halls.

It was a matter of coincidence and logistics that he departed from the very same rustic and tiny railway station in Devon from which I used to return to boarding school some forty years ago. My parents would fondly kiss me goodbye, and my late mother would remind me to send a postcard on arrival, some twenty-five miles distant, to reassure her that I had arrived safely.

Here we were, farewelling my lad to Istanbul. 'Take care, lad, give us a ring in a month or so,' … so has the pace of life moved. (I hope you don't think the Brit Rail diesel car was going from Budleigh Salterton to Turkey that evening, or any other evening. He had forty-two changes and a fourteen-hour journey ahead of him … to London, for a start.)

Well the point of this chapter is that we (dad and son) embraced in a goodbye on the platform, and, in doing so, the paternal hug resulted in a significant crunch – his $300 'very cool shades', i.e. ludicrously expensive sunglasses, hanging on a cord around his neck became 3p worth of broken glass between our manly chests.

Britain 1986

The sign was meant to read: "In case of emergency, phone police here." This was in an English village, affixed to the porch of the one-man police station, manned only from 9 a.m. to 5 p.m. In fact, half the letters had dropped off, and the advice given was: "In case ergency one ice her." I was not surprised, because wherever I went in Britain in 1986 there was a great profusion of incomplete signs. Some were incomprehensible, "–W-TL-B VE—S" being the way one prosperous-looking firm chose to keep its name before the public on the marble slab at its gate, while another, less advertising conscious, was content with "— —'S". Some, like a crossword puzzle, could be worked out from clues supplied: "OGHAM -O-F C-U- (Green fees £2)", or a long queue of stationary cars outside a gate let you know that the "-AR -AR-" was full. One apothecary had me wondering how a shop did business in halves, for he had a proud sign, "HEMIST", but I stared wordless at his neighbour who was a "RAPER". A few rather spoilt the fun by having most of the letters present but some hanging sideways by one nail, so that any fool with a flexible neck could decipher the message. Much rather use glue, so that the whole thing drops cleanly off.

And then there was the machine which is used to burn road markings off the road. You've seen the idea, like a huge blowtorch; lots of tarry smoke and fumes as they patiently scorch away, inch by inch. This was happening in the main street of Dover, where I chose to browse in a large bookshop. It was a warm day, the doors pegged open, and in drifted the smoke off the road, all around those little red things in the ceiling. Presently alarm bells clanged. The bookshop staff were about to act on their fire drill training – but then you could see them pause and think. To try and ease the burden of their obvious quandary, I said, 'It's alright, it's coming from outside.'

They hesitated, reflecting. Logic nearly won the day, but just failed. We were herded out, into the smoke. It was like the Titanic, only the wrong way round.

And then there was the little old lady in her moped crash helmet with a long transparent visor which reached nearly down to her chest. She was lashing her groceries onto the carrier of her vehicle while talking animatedly to another female gnome in a space helmet. What enthralled me, and I stood at her shoulder to be sure, was that the visors effectively reduced the sound of their voices to a scarcely audible squeak, and they were both able to talk at each other simultaneously and without stopping, with no fear of interruption or contradiction. What tremendous advances and advantages science has given us. Hours of conversation reduced to exactly half the time by a piece of perspex!

Later, I discovered that the majority of the twenty-eight million little old ladies in Britain rode speedy mopeds, and in the most devastating traffic. But there were others. My wife and I, behind schedule one evening, put up for the night at a rather peculiar hostelry deep in the wilds of Sussex. It was ramshackle, having obviously seen better times. Rabbits sat brazenly nibbling weeds in overgrown rose beds. We had to pull on a chain and wait minutes before the massive front door opened with creaks and groans. For all that, we had a decent room. After a shower we went downstairs to tackle a steak or two. The first three mouthfuls had gone down, when the courtyard outside was filled with roaring motorbikes. Huge machines with thundering exhausts and gleaming chromium, their riders spacemen in black leather suits, black helmets, black goggles, black gloves.

'We're going to be done by a bikie gang,' said my wife, voicing my alarm. We couldn't get up and run. They trooped in, each one ponderous and sinister, slapping a gross black leather thigh with a huge black leather glove; thirty, forty of them, filling the room entirely. This, I thought, is a Hitchcock script, and I wish I was watching it on the telly. Baleful black goggles looked down on us, robots with no feeling, no pity. My steak was already ashes in my mouth. Then the king robot began taking his head off. It unzipped at his neck and up came the helmet and goggles. Inside was a little bald man, about sixty, with weak watery eyes and a high-pitched voice through loose false teeth.

'Ee by gum, Mabel,' he said, addressing his first lieutenant, 'that were a champion ride from Chichester, but a bit too far for me these days.'

Mabel revealed herself as a shrivelled face with frizzy grey hair, who berated Ada, another demon off her charger, for not bringing the cocoa flask in. As it turned out, the youngest and most vicious of the lot was a retired stamp dealer from Accrington.

Britain 1986; you can't tell an apple from its skin.

Waterworks and Waterways Troubles

I am now continuing my saga of success and popularity in the UK, whither we had landed by courtesy of those clever chaps who fly jets with calm assurance.

Somewhere over Greenland on our way home the pilot came on the air to say, 'Hello, girls and boys ...' (I at once cringed. I would rather be addressed 'dirty old men and women'. Incidentally, are there any dirty old women?) '... We have had a minor malfunction in one engine. We have shut it down and so we'll be a bit late arriving in LA.'

As if to prove the point, an officer with lots of rings on his sleeve came downstairs and peered through the window in front of us at the inboard port engine which (I had already checked because I am such a neurotic flyer) was already stopped.

I then sweated blood, gripping the arms of my seat for seven and a half hours, wondering if the pilot knew how to land it crabwise on three engines. He did, and then told us we must change to a new plane because this one would take some time to repair.

Don't forget all this was for a 'minor' malfunction. What do they do for a major one … saw the wing off?

Brand new

Well, we changed planes to a veritable brand new one, and taxied out onto the runway, turned around, and … no, there was no boooooom and away. The pilot came on the air again – not the same guy, but another who knew about my antipathy to being addressed as a juvenile – and announced, ladies and gentlemen, that there was a fault in the water system which would need an hour 'or so' to repair.

Because we had cleared customs we would have to stay on the plane until it was repaired. Which we did, with the exception of my better half who required to go to the loo before an hour was up, and because of the customs etc. etc. actually had an armed guard march her two miles back along the runway for the necessary.

I, meantime, forgot all about the significance of why we were standing on the runway, and popped along for a quick pee in an off moment. Doubtless there is a Boeing technician in Los Angeles who doesn't like me very much now.

Restricted waters

Our other transport confusion was when we hired a boat to cruise on the Norfolk Broads, something we had done once before, but that had not lent us any great skills in navigating these restricted waters.

We were trying to navigate under the bridge which carries the motorway at Yarmouth, a point where the waterway also connects with the open sea. It was here that I, who was steering, became the only known skipper to totally misinterpret the signs and signals at the bridge, so that we nearly rammed and sunk a seagoing passenger ship which had right of way and came charging through across our bows, as we old sea dogs have it.

All the while the control man on the bridge console jumped up and down in an orange suit like a landing officer on the old aircraft carriers, showering me with abuse and waving his arms like someone demented.

Before we left Norfolk, I was pleased to take part in what my elder daughter calls 'twitching'. For those ignorami among you, 'twitching', in current UK parlance, patois or vernacular, is watching rare birds which have temporarily landed in odd spots. All the *cognoscente* gather with their videos and telescopes to record the event.

Empty section

Well, we were driving along the seafront in Hunstanton when we noticed a bunch of bods with all their equipment on the pavement facing an empty section between two houses.

I grabbed the binoculars and, somewhat to my wife's embarrassment, mobbed in amongst them. I could see nothing, but my ardour was in no way dampened; I made many erudite and appropriate comments to those around me: 'Good Lord.' ... 'Well I never.' ... 'Well I never did.' ... 'Look at it, will you?' ... 'This has made it worth our journey from Tisbiscu.'... 'Of course, we see quite a few albino varieties at home.' ... 'Where's that, mate?' ... 'Tokyo'.

I never saw a thing; I wasn't sure if we were

watching a bird or a butterfly, and I suspect a number of the crowd were equally ignorant, because I picked up no clues at all. Three days later we read in the local press that it was, in fact, a lesser spotted twistle whistle warbler from Leningrad, now known as a St Petersburg Spotty.

Homeward Bound

I am writing this at 600 mph, 37,000 feet above the Pacific, some 800 miles out from LA towards Honolulu – or so the captain of Air NZ 747 'Tainui' tells us. I have total trust in these wizards to navigate me across the whole Pacific during the night, but I wouldn't blame him if he drew the figures off the top of his head – who would really know if we were actually at 37,000 feet or thirty-seven feet, except his cronies in the wheelhouse?

Ahead, and to my right, also at 37,000 feet, and effortlessly maintaining 600 mph, are a bunch of what I call tail toasters. These gentry in aeroplanes are young bloods, including some who think they are young, who spend the flight crouched on their seats, facing rearwards, to hold court with their cobbers in the row behind, and, indirectly, with no subtlety, with everyone else. Usually wearing jeans and a sweatshirt bearing 'UCLA' or 'Steinlager' motifs, or just plain simple Manawatu RC. (My daughters, who live in London, tell me this is de rigueur uniform for all young male

Kiwis in Britain.) They use the headphones to listen to old *Goon Show*s and laugh uncontrollably at each other when the headphones fuse them all simultaneously. Singly, on their own, they derive no happiness from the electronics at all, and take them off until their mates return from the loo queue. At other times, good luck to them, they chat up the hostesses and fill up with more Steinlager. I don't mind all this except for the rearward-facing faces. I think there is a powerful case for the airlines arranging one row of seats in a circle, but then I suppose it would spoil their fun. I can't tell who these particular guys are. At the time of writing, the Commonwealth Games, the rowing and the swimming have all recently concluded, and I see Glen Turner from the cricket a few rows behind me, while to my relief, Dave Gerrard followed us into the plane. I haven't seen him since, in tourist class – perhaps sports medicine pays better than general practice. (I say to my relief because, if any passengers are ill, they are bound to ask him first; no one knows my face except my Golden Kiwi ticket seller. And because if I'm ill in-flight, he can treat me.)

But the best is this, and I make no bones about it. My hypothalamus is not what it was. When I took leave of my daughters in London and my aged mother, whom I don't expect to see again, I entered the plane with prickly red eyes and a stoppage in the throat of a monstrous degree. A Kiwi steward took my bag of duty free, and, stowing it in the overhead locker said: 'Glad you brought that, sir. We ran out of grog on the way over, and haven't had time to restock now, so we'll use yours, if you don't mind, sir, and just supply the soda water.'

My wife says my face was a study. She ruined her prolapse keeping a straight face herself, and I was so distraught I was believing the man. And then I didn't. I burst out laughing through the tears, and I thought, you silly twit, I love Kiwis, you couldn't get that on Air Anything Else.

A Tenuous Connection

It's not that I'm parsimonious, I don't think I am, but I cannot for the life of me see why it is necessary to own more than two or three pairs of shoes. You can't wear more than one pair at any one moment.

It is prudent to have a reserve pair in case the first one gets wet or is otherwise *hors de combat*, and possibly a third of a different colour – although the current fashion of grey seems to be acceptable, at least in the minds of the wearers, at any time, in any combination. I was going to say even with a dinner jacket, but then these are almost extinct now.

Indeed, it almost seems as if suits are the stamp of a pre-war doctor. I have seen colleagues up north going about their practices in thongs, shorts and a T-shirt, while their equivalents down here, on the cooler mainland, wear thongs, jeans and a leather motorcycle jerkin over the T-shirt.

Well suited

My own two sons possess a suit; one suit, that is, between two young men, one of whom lives in Queensland (that's in Australia), and the other in Canada, north of USA. They share this suit, and it will be clear to the dullest intellect that the modern young male Kiwi does not find a heavy demand for wearing a suit when I tell you that they have never needed it simultaneously, nor even so close together in time that transfer of the suit by surface mail has not sufficed. They also have a tie, or they had, but I suspect it was ceremonially destroyed after younger son's capping, since neither of them could envisage any possible further use for it for the rest of their lives.

The first suit I owned was dark blue with a thick chalk stripe, three piece and very natty. I was inordinately proud of it and wore it on all possible occasions, including the evening dinner party for young ladies and gentlemen put on by a lady friend of my mother's for her daughter.

Never the twine shall meet

In those days (soon after the Battle of Hastings) it was customary to keep the trousers up with a pair of braces, but on the night in question I had left things a little bit late and, search as I may, I couldn't find my braces. Having no adjacent male relatives to borrow from, improvisation was the need, and I chopped a piece of garden twine off the roll and tied it to the buttons at the back of my strides, then over my shoulders to the front where I did likewise. My mother was horrified. 'What happens if someone sees?' she said. 'I should be the scandal of the neighbourhood.'

Why she didn't include me in the gossip columns I wasn't sure, but with little time to go into the niceties of the thing, I assured her that no one would know because the waistcoat would hide the string, and it was unlikely, if I knew my mother's friend, to be one of those parties where the waistcoats came off.

And I was right. The waistcoats did not come off. But the buttons did. It was near the end of the evening when, had we been real adults, the port and cigars would have been appearing, but we were suffering cherry cider and coffee, and I was feeling pretty expansive, noting with a certain smug satisfaction that there were only two other suits present and they looked suspiciously like grey school Sunday jobs, not the man-of-world dark blue chalk stripe ... and I had inserted my thumbs in the waistcoat pockets in approved adult fashion, when I felt the buttons ping off at the back of my waist, and the twine around my shoulders go uncomfortably slack, as did my trousers in front.

No remedy

Now if you consider this problem, you will realise that there is no instant remedy. Not, that is, without partly disrobing. Had I used the twine as a belt, and it had parted, I could have surreptitiously drawn it tight again and somehow reknotted it. But the way it was now, the wretched string was halfway up my back, and even if I could have got it down, there was no way of reattaching it to the garment whence the buttons had popped.

In theory I suppose I could have undone it at both its attachments in front, threaded it around my waist under my waistcoat and tied it to act as a belt, but when you consider the setting, and if I recall correctly,

I was speaking at the time, with all eyes upon me, including those of my hostess and her mother, such manipulations under my clothes would have been received rather stonily.

Well anyhow, I was alright as long as we continued to sit at the table, but it occurred to me that I, for one, couldn't sit there all night, and I was stuck for a plausible excuse to sit there after everyone else left the room. In the event, we all sat there until it was time to go home, and then filed out into the hall, to shake our hostess's mother's hand by the front door and away into the night.

How did I manage it? Well, it was simple really. As I rose from the table, taking care to be last, I kept my hands on my hips, clamping the trousers to my waist, a rather odd posture but not one blatantly bizarre. I reckoned I could maintain an up trou status with one hand just long enough to shake the lady's hand, and indeed I would have, but I didn't realise all departing guests were being given a small present, and as she shook my free hand I had no alternative but to use my other hand to receive the gift. Naturally, therefore, my trousers fell to my knees, suspended at the level for all to see by garden twine.

'Thank you very much, Mrs Ellersley-Mainwaring. I do apologise about my trousers. Goodnight.'

The only connection this had with what follows is that on both occasions the audience was not ready for what was said. Recently I was visiting the home of a patient of mine in the terminal stages of cancer, an unhappily familiar scene to us all. He had just come out of hospital, where the experts had been doing some tests in the forlorn hope that salvage might be possible at the eleventh hour. I had not received their report and was questioning the patient, but without much joy because he was so very deaf. My raised voice was clearly audible to his spouse in the next room, where she seemed to be fiddling with the TV, and so she came into the bedroom.

'It's terrible news,' she said.

'Oh dear, I'm so very very sorry,' I replied, to which she responded:

'Wright's out for three.'

Jim

Professor Jim is head of the Blood Transfusion Unit at the city's base hospital. That is his real name and not surprisingly everyone calls him Jim. He once paid me the compliment of offering me a part-time post in this most prestigious unit, when I had retired from General Practice, but for a variety of extraneous reasons I was unable to accept.

This little tale, which is true, may go some way to illustrate the esteem in which the Unit in general and Jim in particular are held by the population it serves. He related it to me himself.

One evening during the winter the hospital received advice that within the next twenty-four hours a woman with one of the dreaded so-called 'flesh-eating' bacterial infections was to be airlifted from a southern province for the intensive specialist treatment needed. Such cases require, amongst other things, enormous and ongoing blood transfusions, perhaps lasting days, and Jim knew that his blood bank, always well stocked for all routine demands, would need urgent and massive extra supplies for this one patient alone. He therefore arranged with the local radio station to allow him to broadcast in person an appeal for all donors of the appropriate blood group to present themselves at his unit by 9 a.m. next morning, if not earlier if possible, but he was aware that a good proportion lived out of town, some as much as forty miles away. The city could provide quite a number but he would need as many as he could get. Thirty donors can donate thirty units of blood but, mindful of this awful disease, he knew that it was possible that he might need thirty units every twenty-four hours.

The message went out shortly before midnight and Jim went to bed for a five-hour sleep.

And while he slept, it snowed. Rarely does it snow much in this region, but it did that night. And then it froze. And then it snowed again. And then it froze again, a most unusual pattern for the city. Rain and wind, yes often, but an arctic night such as this had turned into was very rare. It continued to snow and freeze until Jim awoke and dressed at 5 a.m. Jim told me the rest himself.

It was impossible to get the car out of the drive, let alone down the two miles to the hospital. The city is built on nine very steep hills; they used cable-cars in the old days, and even on mildly frosty mornings many commuters have difficulty in getting to work on time, if at all.

'Well it's downhill so I'll walk' ... but it wasn't to be as easy as that. In the half light of street lamps he stumbled, staggered, fell, slithered, slid, the whole process taking tedious minutes to cover a couple of hundred yards or so. And every now and then it snowed some more. Eventually he reached the flat ground of the city centre, where the going was easier but not easy, and allowed him to ponder more on the situation in general than his own preservation on the hilly slopes. By then it was going on 6 a.m. and in normal circumstances there would have been a few people about: milk and paper boys, early workers, the odd taxi. Today there was no one. There were no tyre marks in the snow on the streets, nor footmarks on the pavements.

Jim reflected sombrely. If he was having a problem traversing only two miles … the conclusion was bleak, and the evidence of his eyes only confirmed this.

'Well, I'll just get there, set up shop and hope that some donors can get to me; but five or ten won't be enough, not nearly enough, not even for starters.'

The street entrance of the Blood Transfusion Unit was separate to, and around the corner from, the main hospital entrance, in a side road. Jim had the keys and while still two blocks away began to fumble for them in his overcoat, his fingers numb and stiff with cold. He said that snow coated his eyelashes so that he found it absurdly difficult to see where he was on streets he trod a thousand times a year. It gave the traffic lights a halo of red, amber and green although there was only he to see them.

On rounding the last corner it appeared that the council had narrowed the pavement; something like an irregular snow-covered tarpaulin lay along the side of the building. It reached from the corner and stopped at the door to the Unit. As Jim peered at it, owlishly, through snow encrusted eyelids, he slowly became aware that it was a queue, two or three deep, of donors of the appropriate blood group, huddled, silent, coated in snow … about two hundred of them …

As he went to unlock the door, a voice from the huddle, 'What took you so bloody long, Doc?', and, from some other, 'I bet she's still in bed though.' A muted ripple of mirth down the queue.

Jim said the egg in his throat prevented him from replying, even if he could have thought of something; and, as he took blood for the next few hours his eyes were not blurred by snow now but tears.

The lady died despite everyone's efforts.

First Catch Your Bird

I dislike killing things which, you might say, is really a rather apposite attribute for a doctor. I suppose, to be strictly accurate, I dislike killing mammals. I swat flies nonchalantly and I fish eagerly – I have never been known to put one back (possibly an unnecessary piece of information for the authorities). But I simply couldn't put down a dog or a cat. It goes against the grain. In fact, so much so that I remember that I gave it as a reason for wanting to be a doctor at my interview for medical school. Actually it came out rather limply with a sense of nativeness about it, if you follow me. My interrogator obviously got the same vibes because he commented guiltily that architects didn't kill things either; then there was something about a board for joining the army or the Quakers which I missed, and I began to feel a distinct sense of relief that my father and my grandfather had both been members of this seat of learning. Old Boy network? We passed from the philosophical to the earthy. He asked, 'What is the difference between these?', and pushed across the table a human skull and a rabbit's skull.

'Ah,' I began, 'one is a human skull and the ...' I caught his eye.

'Name the salient points of difference.'

'The space available for the brain is much bigger in the human skull. Well, proportionately bigger.'

'Go on.'

'In the human skull the eyes look out to the front. The rabbit's ones look sideways. Separately. People don't look sideways. Well, I mean, their eyes look ... er, at you. When you're in front.'

'And if you are not in front?'

'I turn my eyes at you. And my neck. I can see you with both eyes at once,' I answered with a trace of desperation creeping into my voice.

'How fortunate for you, young man. Would it not be simpler, as some would have it, to say that the human skull exhibits frontal binocular vision?'

'Yes,' I said gratefully.

'More!'

'Yes. Well the teeth ...' – this was an easy one, why hadn't I thought of them before. 'The teeth are quite different. In the human being they are for biting and chewing ...' (This came out too quickly and wasn't quite what I had meant to say because I realised what I was going to say next –and so did he.) '... and in the rabbit they are for ... um, ah ... eating.'

Well there must have been applicants who didn't even know that because I gained a place at medical school and went on to expand my knowledge and philosophies until, inevitably, I exuded liberalism and avant-garde thinking, and all the things that in these days would be cool and upmarket – socialism, free love, cappuccino coffee – they were all on. So it was equally inevitable that when the professor of medicine, on a ward round, asked what we thought of euthanasia, I naturally piped up and said I was all for it.

'Yes, sir,' I said, 'People with incurable illnesses who are suffering, it's only kindness and common sense to put them to sleep, no doubt about it.'

I slightly regretted the last phrase because it rather implied that the prof hadn't given it much thought, and I hoped he wouldn't remember when I applied for his house job.

'That's very interesting,' said the mighty man (so perhaps I'd be OK for his job after all). He dropped his voice, 'Tell me, Master ...' (He had a curious habit of calling all medical students 'master' – Master Smith, Master Roberts, Master Williams – and, like all great men, suffered neither a twitch of the eyebrow nor a dent to his dignity when he thus addressed a friend of mine called Bate on ward rounds one day.)

'Tell me then, the man in the end bed, he has multiple sclerosis, he fits your category don't you think?'

'Well yes, yes he sort of does but I didn't mean HIM.'

The prof didn't hear me.

'Sister, would you be so kind as to ask one of your nurses to lay up a tray bearing a fifty cc syringe, sixteen gauge needle, spirit swabs and ten bottles of morphine sulphate. The master here, erstwhile Hippocrates, is going to euthanise the patient in the end bed for us.' He turned back to me. 'I am not sure of the protocol here. Would you like us to remain in the ward, or would you prefer us to go into the corridor while you kill him?'

So when it came to bumping off a couple of our roosters for the pot, my resolve, not to say courage, had been undermined those many years before. We hadn't had chickens all that long and my appreciation of keeping hens extended only as far as distributing grain with a courtly gesture, of an evening, and gathering eggs from the nest.

Now we had too many male birds and they were starting to fight.

'Wring their necks,' my wife said.

Now I've never actually seen anyone wring a chicken's neck. It tends to be one of those phrases which is more of a cliché than a school certificate subject. Everyone knows what you mean, but have you ever met someone who has seen it done, let alone been an expert wringer themselves? Take it from me, neck-wringers are a scarce breed, and I was unable to contact one, so I had to apply basic principles. As in wringing clothes dry, hold the chicken by the neck and … wring.

But first you have to catch your bird, and this took me half an hour and much temper, until I achieved my object only with the help of a length of strawberry netting and a walking stick. Whereupon my spouse, who had been leaning out of an upstairs window, watching, brayed with mirth, 'One up for the bloody gladiator!'

Then I wrung its neck. The chicken unwrung its neck, and looked appealing at me. Steeling myself and looking away, I wrung it again; twice this time. It unwrung, twice unwound. Third try and I turned and turned, and turned, a cold sweat breaking out on my brow. It unwound effortlessly. One final effort. Seventeen full revolutions, then I dropped it. Allow 2.6 seconds and it was pecking grain. I retired from the hen run, temporarily defeated. I entered it again ten minutes later with a brilliant idea and the hedge clippers – which were the brilliant idea. Just sidle up to the bird, casually, and then make a swift CLIP CLIP and, voilá, *poulet au gratin* (hard cheese for the hen).

Now you wouldn't think that an animal, or in this case, a bird, would recognise hedge clippers for what they are, even less for the unusual purpose that I had in mind. Had I sidled up to it with a flower vase or a bicycle pump, I'm quite sure it would have exhibited mild interest and gone on pecking. I doubt that it would have taken umbrage had I carried a pair of skis or a vacuum cleaner, but the hedge clippers were recognised at once for what they were, and I couldn't get within fifteen yards of him. Right then, the gun. I don't possess one, but my partner does and I hopped off to borrow same.

'How many bullets d'you need? How many roosters to bump off?' he said.

'Two,' I said. 'One for each bird.'

He laughed, doubting Thomas, and gave me six.

It was quite simple really. I rested the gun on the gate post, and when one of the roosters walked past, I pulled the trigger. Genius will out, because when the smoke cleared and the commotion died down, there were two roosters lying dead in front of me. They had been kind enough to walk past in opposite directions at the exact moment that I fired the shot cleanly through each eye. I returned the other five bullets to my colleague.

'Thanks, old man, it was a clear day you know.'

Hazy Days

I have never been one for keeping a diary, at least not since I was a callow youth or even younger. Indeed, I had forgotten that I ever kept a diary until I was clearing out an old box in the attic recently. Out tumbled two or three of these very pocket ones, so small that the entries could not be long and erudite and, my word, they weren't.

You may say that the size, or lack of it, would induce in the writer the ability to paraphrase or summarise par excellence by necessity; we would have to have the nub or RES without any frills. And so we did, although, at times, the reader must feel that either my life was incredibly humdrum or else I had honed the message to less than the bones. I quote: "Nothing interesting happened today." What could be more concise? And, next day: "Overcast weather." Nutshell stuff. Later in the week we get: "Pretty ordinary day", followed by "Hot in the sun". To the persistent researcher, it soon becomes clear that like so many of the Anglo-Saxon breed, I was, from an early age, obsessed with the weather, and "Hazy day today" with "Slightly less hazy today" will be valued by any meteorological office. The following Monday's "Slightly cooler – I think" will throw them into spasms of delight, I expect. However, at other times I have more specialised messages to impart.

There is the matter of the knife box. In the course of carpentry lessons at school, I began to construct a box with partitions, eventually aiming to line it with green baize, and keep cutlery in it – or rather for my mother to keep cutlery in it. And so we get the birth of a saga which was to last for some time, in the form of progress reports each week. "Knife box started", "Knife box getting under way well", "Knife box well ahead", "Very pleased with knife box". At this point the intrusion of an inevitable "Nothing much doing today", but we soon pick up the zest with "Put in extra time with knife box, wizard". But then comes the big day, the black day as it turned out, wherein: "Assembled knife box, not at all good, in fact nearly all parts will have to be remade." Apparently this brazen honesty sapped my reserve for knife boxes because they don't figure at any point again in the diaries.

What seems to take over is the emergence of a medical flavour, the first such being "I am afraid I've got mumps as am a bit soor(sic) under ears", followed next day by "I certainly have got mumps". Such was my clinical perspicacity even at an early age. The remainder of the year, and the next two, is taken up with more material for the weather men interspersed with how tired I felt. This comes in various forms: "Am very tired today", "Did nothing today, weary" and "Awfully exhausted now", and I find this very interesting because I always feel tired now but I had forgotten that it must have been a lifelong thing, and had I revised these little booklets sooner, I should have eschewed a career and merely gone onto sickness benefit after School Certificate was over.

Be that as it may, I had enough strength to spend an inordinate amount of entries on my dislike of piano lessons which perhaps occupied a half hour per week but on reading the ongoing diatribe one gets the impression that they lasted all afternoon every day. There is also a solitary entry: "Dr Bilsworth (the botany master) annoyed me intensely in form today." There is no elaboration but from the cold fury of the ink I have the feeling that later in life I was meaning to murder him – but I've forgotten to. I know I didn't like school because I recorded that I went and bought my train ticket home, a journey of all of thirteen miles, a full fortnight before the end of term. 'Be prepared' was the motto. Finally, I couldn't let the holidays arrive without one more entry, and this time with an explanatory rider: "Nothing special happened today … just about average sort of day."

The last diary was from my penultimate year at medical school, and took the form largely of an appointment book, a considerable improvement on the constipated execration of my school days. In fact there are few entries, but one which sounded fun is "Tea with Ann, coffee with Vivienne, broken front spring", and another betrayed my deep interest in sport with "Tea with Vivienne, dinner with Ann, boat race think Cambridge won". The prize for enigma, which remains totally mysterious since I have never known anyone or anything connected with it, is "Lima, Peru, 9.15 p.m. on 26th". And of course no tome by me would be complete without "Lounged around, nothing doing, very weak".

Click Go the Shears, Boys

It wasn't until I settled on a four acre block in New Zealand that my education in sheep began. I acquired eleven of them, a motley bunch, even to my unpractised eye, but as they were only two shillings (10p) each I felt that I could afford risk. There were eleven because I was told that one gauged four sheep to the acre, and the chap selling them only had eleven. I can tell you I felt pretty proud of my flock (or mob, as the local vernacular has it).

But came the day when they clearly needed shearing, So I purchased some hand shears (blades, to us sheep men), set about it rather as a barber would cut hair, snip here, snip snip there, and the results were disastrous. It took me a whole day to do half an animal, leaving it for the night looking like a male lion with an enormous mane. And when I did the head end, my seven-year-old daughter suddenly shouted, 'Daddy, you've cut off her eyelashes', and burst into tears. I reflected better her eyelashes than something at the other end because this 'her' is a 'him'! ... but I had to admit I wasn't up to it. My results were like topiary, the herd looked grotesque and the finely chopped wool valueless, and it was with relief that I learned of a professional shearer and telephoned him to offer him my business. You will notice from the forthcoming dialogue that he was a native New Zealander and used the patois which was not on the curriculum of the British public school which I had attended.

'Hallo,' I said, 'is that Mr Allen?'

'Too right, mate, call me Trev.'

'Yes. Good. Good morning, Trev.'

'Giddaye.'

'I understand you shear sheep. Is that so?'

'My oath.'

'Eh? I beg your pardon?'

'My oath.'

'Your oath?'

'Spot on.'

'Oh, I see. I think I do. You mean that you do shear sheep. Well I have some sheep.'

'Good on yer, mate.'

'Yes. Yes, good on me … but what I mean is they need shearing. I wondered if you could oblige?'

'Jake.'

'What?'

'She'll be jake.'

'Eh? I said I have some sheep and …'

'Yeah, yeah, I heard. Well me best gang's up country for another month, an' there's two jokers short on me other bunch till Tuesday week.' He went on, 'You got rousies?'

'Rousies? Er, no, I don't think so. I believe mine are Romney Crossbreds.'

'Don't get funny, Mister. ROUSIES – to pick up the wool and sweep. Well it'll cost if you want me to bring 'em as well. Tuesday week, then?'

'Yes, oh yes, that would be fine, thank you,' but another thought was now occurring to me.

'And also, Mr Allen, Trev, I am not sure that we'll need a whole gang. How many men do you have in a gang?'

'There's five in me second bunch.'

Two and one fifth sheep per man. Plus rousies.

'Ah yes, as I thought. Yes, well perhaps half a gang would be ample; Well, say two men … or one?'

'Owe big's yer mob, Mister? We can't do a thousand or two in less than a week with only a couple of hands.'

'No, I'm sure you can't. Well don't worry, my mob is less than a thousand. Considerably, er, less. Quite less in fact. Indeed.'

'Two hundred?' The tone was unmistakeable.

'Not quite. Less, in fact.'

'Twenty?'

'Well, getting on that way. Partly.'

There was a pause. I thought I could hear Trev breathing.

'OK, sonny. What's its bloody nime?'

In the event it was a neighbour who did the job, rather surprisingly a retired professor of history who had included high country mustering and shearing in a varied and colourful life. My mob were clean and cool for the summer, the object of the exercise, but also he urged me to sell the wool, saying the proceeds could feed the hens for a fortnight or more; even the dirty dags would fetch a few pence. (Dags are the nasty smelly bits from the 'other' end.)

I explained this to my wife, and she brayed with mirth. 'What's the matter?' I said, 'You wouldn't laugh if it was to fetch twenty quid and I gave you half for your tapestry.'

'Yes, dear, that would be nice, but I was thinking of you going to a wool store to sell that little heap of scraps. It would be like taking a bag of apples to sell at Covent Garden.' Of course her scorn only strengthened my determination, and next day I loaded up my clip, as we sheep men call it, onto the back of my little pick-up truck and set off for the wool store.

In no time at all, I knew my spouse had hit the mark. It was more like one apple to Covent Garden. Have you ever been in a wool store, those huge hanger-like buildings covering eight or ten acres, containing between a quarter to half a million bales of wool, each bale containing sixty fleeces on average? At one end of the store is an office and a mammoth weighing machine. You drive in the 'IN' entrance, and it had been my hope and intention to drive briskly in, weigh, sell, and away home. However, there was a queue of lorries waiting to disgorge their loads, not little pick-up trucks like mine, but twenty-six wheeler behemoths, carrying upwards of sixty bales each, and towing trailers of another thirty bales. Instead of exhaust pipes they had huge funnels which stuck up behind their cabs, and squirted great gouts of black diesel smoke whenever they inched forward as the queue moved on. My heart quaked at the spectacle and I would have run home with my tail between my legs and admitted Elizabeth's wisdom to her face.

But it was too late, already one of these leviathans filled my rear vision mirror and I realised that I was already part of the queue. It was Trev all over again. My eleven fleeces would not constitute even a quarter of a bale, AND they were stuffed in an ignominious old potato sack. The driver sitting eight feet up in his cab behind me would be looking down on my miniscule vehicle bearing its wretched offering; and then I remembered the dags as well. They were in a big paper bag. A paper bag. Oh Lord, swallow me up.

There was a rumble of horse power and a cloud of diesel as the giant ahead of me moved up to the office; the gang of unloaders swarmed over the load, letting go ropes and expertly tossing the bales onto the monstrous scales which could weigh up to twenty tons at a time.

I pondered whether to pretend that I was a detective from Interpol tracking a spy dressed as a lorry driver, or even an Inland Revenue inspector trying to catch out farmers, but before I could explain my policing role I was beckoned forward and the unloading gang, well one of them, leapt onto the back of my cottonreel lorry and threw my pathetic offerings onto the giant scales, the needle of which quivered slightly but without a magnifying glass I was unable to read an actual figure. The tally clerk then emerged from the office and it was on my lips to quote my jumbled brain that I was a spy from the Inland Interpol dressed as a Revenue driver when he mercifully took the initiative. Handing me a bit of paper, he said:

'There you are, sir. One part-fadge mixed crossbreds, one tenth bin dags, one hundred and thirty six pounds six shillings, less handling and auction fees, one hundred and twenty two pounds exactly. What a good way to pay your rates, sir, and a Johnny Walker before bed, too, if it was me. Thank you for your custom, the cheque will be in the mail within two days. Good day to you, sir.'

All the way home I revved my engine at traffic lights, imagining a great black puff of smoke coming out of the exhaust.

'How was it?' Elizabeth's face was tactfully expressionless.

'Not bad.' Insouciance. 'Not bad at all. My part-fadge sold well, of course, something over a hundred, I believe, and the tenth bin another fiver or so. They're sending the cheque. In fact I quite got the impression that they were glad of my custom, the smaller growers perhaps lend a personal touch, something like that.'

And I whistled carelessly.

(PS: Any farmers and accountants among my readers will have registered that that was a very good year for wool growers!)

Sadie

'Mrs Cook, will you go, please go, find yourself another doctor, I've told you repeatedly I can do nothing to help you, we do not see eye to eye, we do not agree on anything, you argue with everything I say, you ignore my advice, you take hours of my time, it's a waste of mine and yours, and I BEG you to change GPs.' As usual, Mrs Cook was unmoved, physically and metaphorically. One doesn't often speak like this to one's customers, in fact I can only recall saying similar once in my entire forty-year practice life to a patient, and to our mutual relief we never met again. But Mrs Cook was made of sterner stuff.

'Och (she was Scottish) you're a sour wee mon an all. Why (now the whining tone) can ye not DO something?'

The only way out was to shoot myself but as I felt an allegiance to my family, not to mention a selfish yearning to live a bit longer, I put the gun away and wearily wrote a prescription for cough medicine for Mrs Cook, the forty-seventh that year, I think.

Of course she was back in a week or two, still chain smoking and still coughing, for which later she held me solely responsible, yay more, she was an aggressive soul and held me to BLAME and never failed to make that clear.

I had inherited her as a patient, as it were. Her late husband had been one of my flock for many years, and married late in life ... to Sadie, whereupon he did the cowardly thing and died, leaving her to me, albeit not in quite the same role, although by now it was making little difference; she was wearing me out. So then I had a brilliant idea. God had smiled, and appointed a new geriatric consultant (did I tell you Sadie was not just aggressive but old aggressive – give me the teenage yobbos any time, in combat) at our hospital and, joy of joys, he too was Scottish. Hitherto any suggestion that 'we' get a second opinion, to take the intolerable load off me and, hopefully, placate Mrs Cook, was met with derision, scorn and blank refusal. 'Yeeure me dorc' (Scottish for 'you are my doc'), 'ahm payin ye', (that bit's obvious), and then would follow a diatribe, none of the words of which I understood but the gist or thrust was 'No', rudely. But here was a fellow ex-pat, from north of the border, one to understand aggressive Scottish widows who chain-smoked and coughed; he might even come from Aberdeen where they smoked herrings and, er, presumably coughed? I cracked that one to Sadie who remained silent, for once, but eyed me with a malevolence which made me check my will that week. However, she agreed to see the great man if only to humiliate me and prove me wrong on all counts. I breathed a sigh of relief, prematurely, as it turned out. The inevitable consultation (with me) the next week: 'Well, what did he say? Could he help?'

'He was a grand mon, nort like yeeeu, but a grand mon.'

I ignored the insults just to get to the pay off. 'Has he cured your cough????'

'Och (Scottish) we neer spoke o tha; he was from Kirkintilloch ... ma horm. Now, aboo ma corf, Dorc ...?'

I couldn't bloody well believe it. Why couldn't he have come from Glasgow, or Iceland, or Berlin or ... words fail me, as they did then. All they did was gossip about scandal in Kirkin-bloody-tilloch and I was condemned to more months, years, of conflict with Mrs Cook's cough. Well I wasn't, as it turned out. Sadie smoked on and on, and coughed until it was hard to breathe and I had to tell her, 'Sadie, I REALLY can't do anything for you this time.'

She said, 'How long, Dorc?'

'Not long.'

I will always remember what she then said – 'Oh boy, oh boy, oh boy ...' – somewhat enigmatic, but that is exactly what she said. She died weeks later.

Four months afterwards a solicitor wrote to me saying that the late Mrs Cook had left her estate to me, and would I mind waiting until her house had been sold before they could send a cheque. I bowed my head.

By the Seat of the Pants?

I suppose I am one of the very few people to have landed a Harrier jump jet while standing up. It was during the Falklands War, and I was serving as Honorary Consultant Surgeon Lieutenant in the flagship.

I was in fact about to operate on the chief engineer for gallstones when the call came. They were desperately short of pilots after the previous day's losses and it was vital to launch one more attack while the enemy were trying to regroup. It would be a chancy mission at best, since the weather was as foul as only the South Atlantic in winter can be, and the range was extreme. Added to that, flying a Harrier is not quite the same as your Cessna 35 back home in the paddock – and I was understandably short of deck landing practice. Only the day before I had said to my chum, the navigator 'Chester', I said, 'I'm dreadfully short of deck landing practice.'

To which he had replied, 'Don't worry, Doc, you're the doc, your place is in sick bay, just leave it to the fly boys and have another gin.'

'Alright' I said, 'but if we get short of them ...' I allowed the innuendo to trail off into my glass. And here we were, twenty-four hours later, with no one to fly wingman to Chubby Gale for what might well turn out to be the *coup de grâce* of the whole war if we could only field a full team.

'Right, I'll go,' I said, 'but I just wish I hadn't started on the chief's gallstones.' (Have you ever noticed how the patients always ring you at home the moment you sit on the toilet, just as if there was a spring-loaded contact under the seat which hooks up with the surgery switchboard. I have actually looked but there isn't one.) I took the clamp off the cystic artery and massaged it until a trickle of blood ran through it, popped in a drain, closed, and dashed off to answer the pipe 'Cooks to the Galley' (lunch in landlubbers' talk) and it was during the meal that I struck a slight snag. I mentioned my proposed temporary change of role, and while most thought it a good – if slightly risky – idea, Torpedo Gunners Mate Robinson asked, 'But what about the Geneva Convention, old chap? The red ring on your sleeve, I thought you chaps had to promise not to bear arms and all that sort of thing?' By Jove, he was right. Medics in the service are only permitted to carry the sword, and a ceremonial one at that, when getting married in dress uniform (the symbolism of which doesn't seem to have struck the feminists yet).

Well, desperate circs call for desperate measures, and in a trice I was wearing the rank and reefer of torpedo gunners mate (second class) and the stirrer was now Surgeon Lt Robinson. 'There's just one other thing,' contributed some other wise guy, 'the others will still call you Doc on the RT when you are in-flight. You'll have to do something about that or Geneva will hear all about it free and gratis over the wireless.' It had to be something short and snappy, and something which would easily roll off the tongue when people were about to say doc and changed their minds. I picked it myself, cleverly I think, although though I say it myself. Dic.

Then we were on the flight deck getting into our cockpits. To say I was nervous was the understatement of the century, but the tension was broken a bit by the deck marshalling officer saying to his petty officer, 'What the hell is that torpedo gunners mate doing getting into Harrier LS14 for? We can't have that,' whereupon his PO (who was in on the switch) smiled, 'It's all right, sir, he's not a TGM, he's the doc, er, – the Dic, I mean.'

The screaming crescendo of the engines drowned all further exchange as we lit up, and soon we were arrowing through the murk towards Stanley and purgatory. I won't bore you with tedious technical details of the bombing run, the rocket attacks, and the ensuing dog-fights, but it all went pretty well except that I lost my long-range tank to enemy flak and so I couldn't go on to boost. This meant dogfighting which, in particular, put me at a disadvantage and it was when I was about to turn for home, having seen all the others safely leave, that I realised that Chubby Gale (to whom I was riding shotgun) was not amongst them.

I had to do several extended sweeps before I found him limping along almost at sea-level on one engine. I waggled the wings in time-honoured signal of recognition and called him up on the RT. 'Hallo, Chubby, it's the Dic here, don't worry, Roger and out.' You could see the relief on his face through the perspex. 'Am I glad to see you, Doc Dic, I'm afraid

I'm a bit slowed down but with you there I'll be OK. Roger and out.'

Well it was a long slow haul. Normally I carry boiled sweets as I suffer from hypoglycaemia between meals but I remembered to my horror that I was wearing TGM Robinson's jacket, ergo no boiled sweets (which doubtless he was now eating) but I felt in the pockets just in case, and yes there was something there. Actually it was just dried prunes, but that was better than nothing, and so I launched into them with gusto.

Then the approach to the carrier. As I think I said earlier I was out of practice but Chubby needed all the help I could give him, on only one engine. The master control from the ship came on the air, 'We see two of you, the rest of the squadron has landed on, so you must be Hellfight Tiger 008 (Chubby's, rather melodramatic call sign – I made a mental not to tease him about it afterwards) and The Dic.'

I corrected the voice, 'It's Dic really, not The Dic.'

They came back on: 'Aren't you the Doc?'

'No,' I replied. 'Well yes, but not now, I'm the Dic! Blast it now you've got me doing it, I'm Dic! Do you read me? Dic, DIC, have you got that?'

'OK, Dic Dic,' said the voice (which I was beginning to dislike). 'These are the coordinates for you to land on, come in on green 41/15 at 132 knots, Hell-fight Tiger 008, and you follow him at the tangential, Doc Doc ... sorry ... Dic Dic.'

Well, Chubby got in just fine and it was just when I was starting my final approach that Robinson's prunes gave me diarrhoea. 'Dic Dic,' came that infernal voice again, 'We think you are going to overshoot.' Little did they know that I had already overshot. There isn't much room in a modern jet bomber cockpit and I didn't want to ruin my parachute, which I might need even at this late stage, so I stood up in a curious half-crouched position.

'Don't worry about coordinates for me,' I told them, 'I've been caught short and I'm coming in NOW!'

Even that they misheard. 'We didn't realise you'd got shot, Dic Dic. Is that why you are standing up? OK Roger, land on land on land on. Over and out. Hey, lower your wheels, Doc Dic!'

It's a very difficult thing to explain in an official report, about the diarrhoea I mean, so I let it stand with them thinking I'd been shot. It seemed nobler somehow, but I was a trifle embarrassed when, on our return to the UK, they asked me to lead the victory parade through London, right from the Guildhall banquet given by the Lord Mayor, down Piccadilly, Whitechapel Road and the Mall to Buckingham Palace where the Queen stood on a plinth to receive our salute. I have to admit that the tears of emotion were hot and stinging in my eyes when I was told that it was the first time in history that the monarch had saluted first. When I got home that evening there were more accolades including a telegram from the PM. "You are a brick, Dic. Well done, Margaret", and my wife answered the phone, 'It's tolls, collect, from Geneva,' she said.

'Forget it,' I replied. 'Don't accept it, I don't know anyone there.'

That's what you get for eating raw oysters and cheese immediately before going to bed.

Worth Every Cent?

It was, I think, 1973 when my wife and I attended the WONCA Conference in Mexico. The conference itself was a mixed bag where, amongst all the undoubted academy, there was a leavening of colleagues who delivered lectures so peculiar that their deliverers must surely have had an eye to their tax-deductible expenses.

Thus, one gentleman from Australia gave us an exposition on his plan for bullet-proof telephone boxes for the Great Outback, something I would have thought more appropriate for King's Cross or, sadly, these days, New Zealand. Another, a Mexican GP, gave a long and very boring account of backache which turned out to be his own (back, I mean, not account, although of course that was his too ...). Perhaps one should not blame him too much for the tedium because he spoke in Spanish which I do not understand and although there was instant simultaneous translation through headphones, the translators spoke in deadly monotones, without punctuation or, apparently, breath, so that the effect was like listening to the commentator on a horse race which never gets to the end. I guess this is the *modus operandi* of all these international meetings and goes some way to explaining why the United Nations makes no progress.

Mind you, we had expected that there would be dull patches, so we had taken the precaution of spending a few jolly days in the United States on our way to Mexico. Have you ever tried to sort American dollar bills out? In case you have not, I will tell you that they are all the same colour and size, whether $1, $2, $5 or *any* denomination, it is only the portrait of the respective president which varies, a vaguely patriotic sort of gesture, and of little consequence to the average native of the States who can tell at a practised glance if Abe Lincoln is the right man for his purchase or whether a couple of Coolidges are needed for a martini. Well, I'm not too hot on my presidents and had to rely on looking closely at the numbers which are printed in very small figures on the notes, a procedure which unintentionally lent me a mean and furtive air when buying anything at all.

The crisis came one night at a Greek nightclub in San Francisco, or Frisco as we men of the world call it. I had consumed well if not over-wisely and during the later part of the night the performance of one of the staff, a hardly dressed at all belly-dancer, impressed me considerably, so much so that I felt constrained to show my appreciation in the usual way. Immediately I explain that that does not mean clapping one's hands in Greek nightclubs; the next time she oscillated within inches of our table, I did the right thing, and pressed a dollar note between the string of her G-string and her epidermis, essaying a paternal smile and nod, which I fear may have come out more of a leer with a wink loosely attached. I must admit that her response was more than I had expected or even hoped for, after which my wife said rather frostily that it was time we were going. There was more ice in the cab on the way back to our hotel, together with a certain amount of muttering about 'thinking he's the last of the big spenders', and at the time I took this to be a sort of feeling of healthy sisterly rivalry; but next morning, when the mists lifted and I commented mildly that tipping was expected in America, I was told, 'Yes, but not $20 a time.' Perusal of the residual wallet contents revealed the awful truth; no wonder the lass had been so pleased – those were times when $20 was $20, or more.

On the other hand, I possibly got more for my money than the American tourist who was in our group when we reached Mexico. We had got as far as Acapulco which, among other things, is famous for its La Perla divers (you may have seen them on ads on TV when you see a superb young man do a magnificent swallow dive from the top of a cliff into the surging ocean hundreds of feet below). Well, in real life a rather past-his-best, if not frankly jaded, Acapulcan does the deed, albeit tolerably well – at least he wasn't killed the time we watched. But where I had expected there to be a troop or platoon of divers at the ready atop the cliff, be they not each an Adonis, it was in fact a one-man enterprise, and the catch to this, if you are not ahead of me, is that having dived into the ocean, he had to swim back to the cliff base, secure a footing without being crushed to a pulp by the swell, and then laboriously climb back up the several hundred feet he has just dived down, get his breath, adjust his trunks, have a brief prayer and then dive off again. The dive takes about three milliseconds and the rest of it a good half hour on days when he's going well. Our American co-tourist looked away for the three milliseconds and so missed out because you are not allowed to stay and wait for the next dive without paying again.

Fandangos and Faux Pas

This isn't meant to be a serial, but it so happens that my train of thought (along the need for good communication in medicine) takes me back to Mexico, about which the *aficionados* of this column will recall I wrote last time.

The biennial WONCA Conference was in Mexico City some years ago and my wife and I spent a week in Acapulco first, getting the feel of the place. Acapulco is humid, by the sea, and very very hot, night and day, so much so I was relieved that I had brought my shorts and wore them from day one. This caused some consternation and enormous amusement to the majority of Mexicans, who are not accustomed to wearing shorts at all, ever, and are only used to seeing people in the Bermuda type garment that Americans wear, something like a pair of ordinary longs cut off at, or just below, knee level. My very Kiwi-type short shorts, offering a lot of the quadriceps to the tropical sun, had them in spasms of mirth and I felt ridiculously heroic for a while, but after a bit I became used to a gust of laughter and a roar of applause whenever I entered a room and quite missed it when we left the country. I suppose this is something like a prime minister feels when he has lost office.

We flew *up* to Mexico City, literally, because it is on a plateau 10,000 feet up and we were leaving the coast. I hadn't really thought about this when we boarded the plane. I am always a very neurotic flyer, listening with dread to every change in note of the engines and interpreting the fact that every steward is not smiling as evidence that the crew have knowledge of impending disaster. So when we had been airborne for about half an hour, with the plane still in a climbing attitude, the engines suddenly cut out and there was a frightful grinding and bumping sound from under the floorboards. As the plane shuddered and bucked, I grabbed my wife's hand, tears of sorrow and terror in my eyes. 'I'm so sorry about everything, I have tried hard, I love you.' (I really don't know what I was referring to but it all made sense at the time, petrified as I was).

'Yes, dear,' she said, 'how nice, but not in public and we get out here anyhow,' whereupon a steward opened the door in the side of the plane and, instead of being sucked out into space, began to talk to someone *outside*. Incredulous, I rose from my seat to see if I could get a view of, presumably, God or at least an angel, in the flesh so to speak, but my gaze was met by ground crew on a ladder staircase which, in turn, was on the ground ... ten or twelve feet below us.

No communication, you see, and so it was also at the grand reception for all the delegates to the conference at what I suppose was the City Hall or something similar – a very imposing building with a massive flight of steps up to a magnificent portico. To get there we had joined one of the fleet of buses engaged to ferry delegates from their hotels. I remember that there were a great many Canadian colleagues and periodically, as the bus drove through the city, these chaps gave vent to a great roar. Their behaviour was explained when I realised that the word *'canada'* means shoe shop or footwear in Spanish, so that they cheered as we passed each shoe shop. Perfectly understandable except that when you reconsider it, it is a bit odd for a country to be called Shoes in anyone's language. Anyhow, we arrived, we were received, we mingled, we sipped fine wines, we chatted, a mariachi band played Mexican music in the background; it was all very convivial and gracious. More mingling, meeting Indians and Germans, more wine and introductions, the music throbbed a bit louder, a glow of bonhomie. We talked and met more Canadians and laughed about shoe shops, and soon a few couples were dancing gently to the evocative strains, so we joined them. My word, how evocative they can get. I didn't think I had Mexican blood in me, but I found I could dance with hitherto undiscovered skills. The band seemed to gather speed and enthusiasm too and my twinkling toes led them on. I executed some amazing pirouettes which my wife found hard to follow but she did a noble job of trying and in the end we were the only couple left on the floor. This really seemed an enormous compliment, as everyone stood quietly and still, watching us in evident awe while we performed a myriad of complicated and breathtaking movements. I'm not an expert but I would have described them as a delicate balance between fandango and rock and roll. Anyhow, it was dashed clever and, anticipating the end of the music to a T, we finished with a flourish. I was not actually expecting applause from such company but I was touched when one of our hosts came up to me with a few sentences of which I only knew 'Señor', and tears in his eyes.

'Thank you, thank you,' I said. 'Not at all, you are too kind.'

Then one of my new Canadian chums, quite a linguist, who was standing nearby, caught my eye: 'I won't tell you what he said, buddy, but if I was you I wouldn't do a Haka to their National Anthem again.'

Not With a Bang but a Whimper

It's never like in the movies, is it? I mean you would be astonished if, towards the end of a murder investigation, the detective mustered all the relatives and suspects in a big room – being careful to avoid a time clashing with the Lotto results on the telly – and went through a step-by-step unravelling of the case with the big dénouement at the end.

Likewise in the theatre world one is inclined to get 'flesh wounds' resulting from gunshot injuries to the thorax, as long as they miss the heart (the chest and shoulders apparently being made up of solid meat which a .44 calibre bullet can only momentarily bruise, like hammering your thumb). Pneumothoraxes don't exist because they would slow down the action so much. Fancy having to put up a water-sealed drain in the desert, or having an actor *very* short of breath because *both* lungs had been collapsed.

So it is with dying. The histrionic death is a scene much beloved of the dramatists, and tolerably realistically performed, I've always thought. I am not referring to the peculiar callisthenics which cowboys perform as bullets riddle their non-fleshy parts (presumably something to do with falling in the best site for the lighting, or giving small boys something to imitate) – I mean falling to the ground shot dead is a non-event.

No, I refer to the classic deathbed scene where the family and friends are grouped around in order of seniority and height, women weeping quietly, men solemn and stiff of lip, while the deceasing subject gives a reasonably succinct abstract of his or her entire life, moving to a relevance to those present, summaries of likes and dislikes, details of the will, and thus the finale with appendices of thanks to individuals and corporations – like a Miss World or Oscar Award – leading up to the winners, the nearest and dearest. There may be a few replies, but these are kept short and the cameras are kept on the principle, who, having truly exhausted his or her vocabulary, looks wistful and peaceful.

Asystole is clean and polite, the head turns to one side, holds for a second, and then the chin falls on the chest as the eyes close. I agree that this very last bit is not very true to life – if that is the correct word – but it is, well, seemly. The nearest I ever saw to the real thing was Laurence Olivier turning his eyeballs up while keeping his eyes open; in anyone else this would have been very convincing, but with him it just looked like Laurence Olivier being clever as usual.

Well now, apart from my very last minor criticism of the scene, what is wrong with this picture? It had never occurred to me before but there is one vital part of the biz – as we theatre people call it – which can and does go wrong. Let me recount to you the facts in a case of mine.

We had the whole cast coming in on their cues beautifully; the patient was a gracious lady with good delivery and an impeccable sense of order. She took hands in hers and squeezed them with a finely judged degree of increasing weakness. Roughly every three relatives I silently moved in to check the failing pulse, gravely shaking my head as its volume fell and its rate increased. More relatives, more monologue. Getting near the end the breath came in gasps. Muted sobs arose from the assembled, and then goodbye, 'No, make it *au revoir*', was said to the spouse, the final VIP. All was said, all was *finis*, and the wistful peaceful look came on. We bowed our heads; more sobs; we kept bowed; a minute of silence passed (except for the sobs); then another minute or two, perhaps three. Through my eyebrows I looked at my patient. She looked fine and was wistful and peaceful, but looking at the telephone as if the call she expected was coming via the post office.

I coughed discreetly and felt the pulse. It was weak – well, fairly weak – running about seventy-six. I drew back again and kept my head bowed. We waited. Someone shuffled their feet and the patient got into a more comfortable position. Well, understandably, one doesn't want to go with cramp. The spouse took a chair, being elderly himself, and I could have sworn that someone tiptoed out of the room. Suddenly the patient sighed and we all looked up expectantly, but she was only sighing. She comforted us with a wan smile.

Quite soon I realised that they were all starting to look at me (through their eyebrows), as if it was my fault. I took the pulse again, and this time nodded to lay the ground for the fact which was becoming most evident, that we were going to have to stand down.

Sotto voce, I suggested that the younger amongst us might like to make some tea for the older, and that I felt it wise and prudent for my patient to be left alone for the nonce – or an hour or two, or perhaps a week. There was an ill-restrained stampede for the door, and twenty minutes later we all dispersed for other climes.

I expect you think I'm going to close by saying that I met the lady in the shopping mall three weeks later, but such is not the degree of my clinical error, nor her timing, and it was in fact four days later that her aneurysm burst as she was on her second plate of porridge, and she was gone in a trice with not a monologue but a rather earthy grunt which her aged spouse took to be approbation of the oats since her mouth was full.

The Expert Witness

I think I have mentioned in these pages before that being a doctor, particularly a GP, necessitates performing in front of the public, and ergo, it helps if you are a bit of a showman.

Be this inherent or acquired, it is never put to the test more openly than on those occasions when we have to appear in court as expert witnesses. Now there was a time, in my far distant youth, when the thought of public speaking terrified me out of my skin. I can remember the occasion when I won a bar of chocolate at a dance when aged twelve, and darted out of the door and away into the night rather than have to go on the stage to receive my prize.

My baptism of fire, after which I felt confident and indeed happy to address the United Nations General Assembly if required, occurred some five years later when I was a senior prefect at a public school of ancient traditions in England. One of these traditions was that the Lord's Prayer be said in Latin in front of the whole school of four hundred boys and masters once a week by one of the senior prefects, taking turns throughout the term. While he did this, the said prefect appeared to read from a hallowed piece of wood, handed down from 1604, on which the Latin words had been recorded.

Well, when my turn came, I took 'the Wood' from its niche, strode up in front of the assembled multitudes, and uttered forth; and, having heard it said every week for the preceding four years, I knew it by heart, so I looked not at the wood but out over my audience:

'*Pater noster, qui es in caelis, santificatur nomen tuum, et veniat regnum tuum, fiat voluntas tua in terris et in caelis ...*' and then I dried up. Silly, really, I could have gone right through to the finish saying it to myself in the bath, but the fright of the moment got to me. However, all I had to do was glance down at the wood to prompt me, which I did, only to see that there was, in fact, nothing written on it at all.

The earth refused to swallow me up, so I mumbled a few garbled Latin phrases which crept to mind, something like '*ipsofactoad hocnon illegitime carborundrum sine que non ad infinitum, Amen*' and, beetroot-faced, strode off the stage.

After that, I find courts are child's play. Mind you, I never fail to get it wrong – I just don't blush. There was the perfectly simple assault case where I had to describe the victim's injuries to the court, and the belligerent lawyer, instead of engaging me in a rapier-like exchange of wits and cunning, asked me what the letters after my name stood for. Well I got my main degree right, but then I have a jumble of lesser diplomas, and I got these muddled in my haste to oblige, and said I had MRCOG when I meant MRCGP and corrected myself, with a winsome smile to the judge, adding that I'd never thought of it before; a somewhat lame statement at which the learned gentleman sniffed.

Then there was the time in the High Court, where you wait in the corridor until called. When I was called I entered the court and what I took to be the witness box, although there was a person whom I presumed to be the last witness still in it. I said to him, *sotto voce*, 'My turn now, old chap, you can skip off.' Actually, this was the dock I had entered and the accused I addressed, a mishappening advertised to the world since I am a short fellow and my mouth was almost level with the microphone concealed in the scroll work of the rather ornate dock. My words boomed around the whole chamber to the delight of the public and the ire, once more, of my learned friend.

'Get out of the dock, you idiot,' hissed the solicitor on our side, to which, before I could catch myself, I boomed again, 'Sorry', all around the building. It's all very well for the legal johnnies who spend all week in the place; I'd like to get them in an operating theatre, and see if my learned associate knew the form without being prompted.

It was the High Court again, and a most unhappy case of alleged rape. However, I had managed to get into the right piece of furniture to do my expert exposition. All was going well, at least from my point of view, until the cross-examining gentry tangled me up in dates – the last period, the maturity of the pregnancy, the assault times. It really sounds quite easy to reckon now, but such is the art of these legal eagles that my mental arithmetic, never a strong point, broke down and I assumed the childish ruse of counting on my fingers with my hands held behind my back, a sort of digital abacus, whenever the barrister attacked me with another chronological teaser. This produced the impression of grave, if slow, thought when viewed from the front, but the jury were sitting behind me, and became fascinated with my manipulations to the extent that, in the end, they began to titter. Of course the learned MC wanted to know why they were laughing and guess who got the pursed lips again.

When I got out, I found I had a parking ticket, and I was so incensed that I went straight round to the MOT and thumped the table with some vigour to the effect that I wouldn't have been late 'if the jury hadn't taken so long to make up their minds'. I was aware that this explanation lacked something, but the gist was enough to imply some sort of catch-22 situation to the officer on duty, and he let me off. I think I'll be a barrister when I grow up.

Honesty the Best Policy

An alfresco lunch at a harbourside pub in Fowey in Cornwall. You know the drill, you go to the bar and give your order and they give you a number, whereupon you resort to a bench outside and inhale fresh air and alcohol while they fry your 'Hameggan Chips'. When ready, this culinary masterpiece is then borne out by a young lady from Australia working as a waitress as part of her European education. She calls a number to the hungry herd of boozers and the lucky one raises an arm and shouts 'Yo' (that is, if you are trendy and with it, like me; the stodgy old farts and the inexperienced shout 'Here' or 'What?').

On this particular day, the young lady's high soprano voice was manifestly failing to get through to the customers, what with a hubbub of chatter and noises from the harbour boats, seagulls and sundry passing ambulances, so being the noble fellow I am, I stood next to her and bellowed out the numbers in stentorian voice, rather like a bingo caller, '444 all the fours'. This was not an entirely altruistic move on my part; the sooner we got the peasants their chaff, the sooner we would get ours. I must admit that, while shouting, it occurred to me that some of the dishes looked more succulent and more expensive than the humble fare we had chosen, and how would it be if I called out *our* number for a surprise gourmet treat? I forbore, but it was the same devious cunning I had exhibited one day when I found a parking ticket under the windscreen wiper of my car. I kept it in my pocket for the next week or two until I paid the fine, but in the meanwhile making very good use of it, slipping it back under the wiper whenever I parked, thereby gaining complete immunity not only in orthodox car parks but also in loading zones and even on double yellow lines. I was very sad when I finally had to part with it, and considered writing my own ticket in its place for free parking in perpetuity, but something told me I might be pushing my luck. I am an honest man.

This being so, when the opportunity to really cash in on my retirement arose, I hesitated and thus missed the moment. It all happened unexpectedly in the following way. After exactly forty years in harness I hung up my stethoscope, and shortly after a number of gifts from grateful patients began to arrive. (Yes, I wondered that, too; were they grateful that I had retired?) Well, never look a gift horse, and they were all gratefully received. The flow dwindled to a trickle, and when it had ceased altogether I'm afraid I did the lazy thing (as well as the fact that I started to get muddled as to who had given me what) and placed a notice of deep appreciation in the local paper. To my astonishment, and not a little embarrassment, in a few days more gifts began to arrive, not quite as many as before but a very significant contribution, and all from those who hadn't given first time round, clearly prompted, reminded or stung by my newspaper notice, or possibly in a spirit of rivalry, not wanting to be outdone by the Joneses. What on earth to do now? I simply couldn't put ANOTHER notice in the paper, that would imply … which just goes to show what poor, naive, non-business-like people doctors are. Speaking about my dilemma to a very worldly businessman friend, I was greeted with pained incredulity.

'My dear chap, what a golden opportunity. What you MUST do now is put another thanks para in, and follow it with some details. The poor folk will want to know how they can please you most. It's like a betrothed couple letting everyone know what wedding presents will go down best.'

'Details?' I said.

'Very much so, viz for a start let them know when your current stocks of whisky will run low; tell them, as you told me, that you have enough Parker pens and jerseys to last you until you are 107; that book tokens are preferable to books they wanted to read but you don't. Have you enough poultry in your deep freeze? Perhaps several of them could go shares on a new lawnmower, one of the sit-on ones as you're retired now; things like that. And then THEN … (he was getting well into his theme now) … Then you make it a monthly insert in the local rag, a sort of ongoing goal for them to aim at, and at the same time you begin publishing the names and addresses of the defaulters, those who have persistently failed to cough up; name and shame; get proactive, man.'

I've never understood what proactive means, as opposed to active, my dictionary is too old to contain the word, but what he said began to make me think it means nasty rich, and I thought I wouldn't tell him how to get free parking.

Interventionism in Obstetrics

My teaching hospital farmed us out to get our practical maternity experience. Dave and I went to Norwich, where we were quartered in a cottage in the hospital grounds, which we shared with an Irish anaesthetist. When off duty, this happy bachelor spent much of his time inhaling impressive quantities of Guinness and regaling Dave and me with detailed accounts of his bedroom exploits.

We were quite agog to hear his descriptions, and I for one wrestled with the mental vision of the pudding-like probationer nurse I had been dating (holding hands in the pictures and a kiss on the nurses' home steps) performing similar hormone-wrenching callisthenics. Idly, I wondered if one was allowed to keep the light on during the procedure, or if that was just too rude and it should all be a tactile experience. And also if I could at least keep my pyjama top on – I had a new set, imitation blue silk, of which I was rather proud.

Anyhow, the purpose of our presence there was to deliver babies. Our cottage was opposite the labour ward, but between the two buildings was a tennis court, surrounded by a sixteen-foot high wire mesh fence.

On our first night in residence, the phone rang: 'Come quick, the head is nearly out.' Keen as mustard, I paused only to put slippers on, and, although it was snowing gently, I added nothing to my imitation blue silk pyjamas, knowing the ward was but a few paces away across the yard. I forgot the tennis court, and in the pitch darkness, I didn't see it. Out of the cottage like a champagne cork, aiming for the lighted ward windows, I passed through the open gate in the fence without knowing it was there, and, running strongly, I had worked up to about 35 mph, before I crashed heavily into the wire mesh on the other side of the court. Winded and perhaps mildly concussed, and very surprised, I got up, brushed some snow off, and began to feel my way round for an exit. Murphy's Law ensured that a gust of wind had closed my portal of entry, and for fifteen minutes I bungled around, cold and cursing, until I knew I should die of frostbite, rather ignominiously. There was nothing for it but to climb the wire! I had to drop the slippers to get a toe hold, and when I did get to the top and got stuck trying to manoeuvre the soft parts over without tearing (the fence was intended to keep balls in, of course), I suddenly found myself illuminated by a powerful torchlight from below. Two or three voices murmured with surprise, one adding, 'We'll have to get more sensible students than this, you know.'

Confessions

I had a young locum once who told me that when he had completed the stint for me, he was going to the States to further his studies and become an oncologist. I expressed avuncular concern, saying that I felt he showed great professional promise and it would be a great shame to waste his skills on in-growing toenails and bunions for the rest of his life, thereby revealing my abysmal ignorance (had I forgotten all my school Latin?) (or ???Greek) that oncology referred to cancer and what my shrivelled brain was confusing with it was the term ungual (Latin, definitely, this time) referring to nail or hoof, although to this day I can't see the connection …

He has never forgotten this, and seldom fails to remind me and bray with mirth, on his few returns to this country. He comes by private jet. When the White House can spare him.

Meanwhile, I prune my roses and comfort myself that both Schweitzer and I have saved lives by correctly diagnosing strangulated herniae.

And then, of course, I was asked to write this column. At once, I went to the completely full, 47 by 112 metre shed in which I keep unopened medical journals, and, at the five-metre mezzanine level, I located them. What I read filled me with awe and humility. To compete with these experts and super-docs? I was instantly reminded of the horrors I suffered when I returned to a reunion of my alma mater. Like many, I presented a talk and slides to qualify for income tax deductions on the trip. Unlike the others, who presented erudite expositions such as 'Radiotherapy and Your Mark VII Betatron', 'How to Recognise HTLV 3 in Rota Extracts', and 'The Quintessence of Quantifying Dystrophics', I gave a chat (I had no option, once I was propelled onto the podium and my slides were being shown) facetiously entitled 'Fat Female Problems'. The slides I had purchased in Soho, the politest of which portrayed naked ladies with fifty-five inch busts, and, perforce, the text of my message had to fit the action shots, of which there were rather a lot.

I get the same feeling at the end of lectures, when questions are invited. I've never asked one yet, quite simply because I know everyone will gape, then roar with mirth. Did you ever have those infuriating mentors, who, when you asked a question, invariably replied, 'Well, what would *your* answer be to that?' I realise they are trying to make me develop my brain, and that was OK when I was twelve, but still it goes on and I've had enough. As a final year student, I suffered this from the Professor, now a peer of the realm to boot, and had I not been mindful of my chances of later getting his house job I would have replied, 'Get stuffed, you stupid bugger.' I wish I had, because I still didn't get his house job.

Out of Place

I have always cherished an eccentric desire to conduct morning surgery or do a ward round dressed in a fireman's outfit – complete with helmet, big rubber boots and an axe tucked into my belt – not to satisfy some wayout fetish urge, but to observe the reaction in the patients.

I think it is very likely that many of them would make no comment at all.

I have a brother-in-law who is able to pass these sorts of things off with a straight face which I probably could not, thus ruining it from the start. He used to commute from Surbiton to London, each day tucked into the same railway carriage with the same city business men, all reading the *Financial Times* and never speaking to each other.

One day he entered the train and sank into his usual seat, nodded as usual to the other inmates, who, as usual, nodded silently back and were about to drop their eyes again behind their *Times*'s when they were transfixed to see Gerald deliberately draw out of his breast pocket a piece of ordinary string with a loop fashioned at one end. The loop he carefully arranged around his left ear, before placing the free end of the string in the corner of his mouth. He then opened his *Times* and began to read.

No one spoke throughout the journey, as usual, and at Waterloo he merely removed the string from ear and mouth, replaced it in his pocket, nodded curtly and got out. He repeated this procedure every Thursday, only on Thursdays, for three months. No one ever asked him why.

Thoroughly tiresome

On another occasion I am told that he spent an entire cruise of the Scandinavian fjords posing as a German, speaking with a gross guttural accent and being thoroughly tiresome, asking British passengers on board if the English beer and weather were as bad as they were reputed to be.

On the day that the vessel returned to Southampton at the end of the cruise, the sun was shining, the sky was blue and the bees were humming, and the Brits were about to disembark when they saw their boorish pseudo-Teuton approaching, and they delayed long enough to point out to him that it didn't always rain in England, to which he replied: 'Me dear chaps, it scarcely requires the perspicacious for one to be aware that it is a perfectly spiffing day and, as Bertie Wooster would have it, God's in his heaven. Toodloo,' and he was down the gangway with a jaunty swing of his tightly furled umbrella.

Mind you, there is no need to go adopting schoolboy devices like guttural accents or black beards and dark glasses if you want to disguise yourself, as I discovered by accident. Just be in the wrong place at the right time.

There are times when my nurse is further away from the telephone than I am, and since I detest the sound of it ringing, I have often been known to lift the receiver and announce my name. Inevitably, without any exception over the last twenty-seven years, the caller instantly hangs up or, at most, says, 'Sorry, wrong number', first. They then ring again and if I answer again they hang up again in 47.3 per cent of cases, and in the remainder an incredulous voice says, 'Is that you, Doctor?' to which I reply, 'Yes, I just said it was I,' and they reply, 'But I didn't think it was you.' Some of these even hang up again at this late stage and ring again an hour later, hoping for the safety of getting my nurse whom they expected all along.

Well, in a way I can understand this, but I was totally unprepared to have my face and whole being denied on another occasion. G K Chesterton has something to say about this phenomenon in *The Purloined Letter* and I have to be gracious and say he thought of it first and didn't crib the idea from me.

My version occurred one day when my car suddenly broke down at home at lunchtime, and my wife had been inconsiderate enough to take hers to work with her. I was two and a half miles from my rooms with a full list of patients to see in about ten minutes' time. Where we live it can take half an hour to get a taxi out from town for starters, and I was about to slip into something light and try jogging for the first time in my life when I though of the children's bicycles, standing unused at the back of the garage this past year or two (since the 'children' are well into their twenties).

Choosing one of the sons' very macho machines, as I felt befitted Father, with handlebars low over the front axle and seat near the stars, I tied my bag on the back, and we were off. It was very exhilarating downhill, but got tougher than I expected on the level. Nevertheless, I made manful progress.

My neighbour ignored me; probably I went so fast he didn't actually see me, I thought. So did the postie. Well, she was probably worried about getting the right letters in the right boxes. I did wave, but still … Then I saw a patient of mine whom I'd only just seen before lunch, sauntering along the street. I waved some more and called out a cheery word. He stared blankly at me. I pedalled on.

It was hot in a suit and tie and I was glad to have to slow down for a pedestrian crossing on which my bank manager, no less, was strolling back from his lunch break. 'Hallo, Frank,' I began, and was about to explain to him in a jocular vein that I was serious about my overdraft to the extent that, ergo, here I was saving petrol, when he cut me dead and walked on. Miserable scrooge came to my mind, resolving at the same time never to save petrol even if he begged me to.

More pedalling. I must say that I was faintly disconcerted when the lady from the Lotto counter failed to respond to my 'Gidday, Gidday' (did I tell you that I have been accepted as a Kiwi citizen at last, but they turned me down for Outer Mongolia – see about eight issues back). I mean my retirement and much of my current near-liquidity is based on Lotto, and she should have broken into smiles at the sight of her best customer.

Crowning event

The crowning event was the district nurse, almost one of the family you might say, who preserved a glassy stare through me despite my halloos and professionally shouted, 'What d'you think of old Aggie's leg ulcers this week?' My own nurse nearly knocked me off the bike in our car park as she swooped in, and when I took her severely to task she just said, 'Oh, I thought you were some yobbo.'

I realise now that I have no need of Lotto. All I have to do is rob a bank, and as long as they let me ride a bike into the bank and out, no one will know who I am.

In the Hot Seat

They were a dear old couple living in a new pensioners' flat, and on the occasion of my visit they took great pride in showing me round and demonstrating how they had managed to condense their furniture from the old house into two and a half rooms.

There wasn't nearly enough space for the old sitting room suite so that had had to go and in its place their children had clubbed together to buy them two very expensive armchairs. These had panels which elevated out from a recess rather like the wing flaps on a jumbo jet. You simply sat in the chair, reached over the side to grasp a wooden handle which, when pulled, brought up the footrest, carrying your feet with it.

At the time of which I write, this was a novel idea, and I needed no second bidding when they urged me to try it out. I sat, I reached over, I grasped, I pulled … and hey presto my feet were involuntarily brought up level with my chest so that I was instantly supine. (I couldn't help reflecting that the oedema in my elderly couple's ankles would be restored to their lungs, whence it had come on getting up in the mornings, and that perhaps now someone should put on the market a bed with a lever which dropped the user's feet for the night, so that they could at least get some part of the twenty-four hours without being breathless at rest.) However, I kept these ruminations to myself and instead gave vent to exclamations of delight and extreme comfort, as was expected of me.

Comfortable

Indeed, it was a very comfortable chair and I had no need to invent emotions, and we chatted on, until I was thinking that it was time to share my presence out with other patients on my visiting list.

I made a move to get up, but it was swiftly apparent that this could not be done from the lying-down position in which I was unless you performed a sort of rolling, diving plunge for the floor, rather like baling out of a stricken Spitfire in the Battle of Britain. Such histrionics I thought unnecessary when all you had to do was work the wooden lever the other way and the footrest would subside. So this I did, and that it did, even as my hosts were telling me to reverse the lever to drop the feet.

Now I don't know who was to blame for what happened next, whether the designers, or the makers, or ACC or me for having unusually muscular calf muscles which bulged inordinately – not that anyone has ever made comment about them to date – but the fact is that, as the footrest descended, it took a bilateral bite on the meatiest part of the each gastrocnemius and remorselessly drew these two juicy chunks of my flesh into the recesses of the chair. And I do mean IN. There were parts of me inside the chair.

Sucked in

The first chair they invent with machinery and I have to get sucked in, literally. And let me emphasise that, when the chair is in the closed mode, there is no space inside. The foot rest fills it snugly, entirely. What we now had was a non-existent space with some of the GP in it.

And let me also tell you that it hurt. Slamming a car door on your finger is a laugh a minute in comparison. If I come to a THR I'll tell the anaesthetist to take the day off. The pain was breathtaking, to the extent that I had been going to scream when my legs met up with my thalamus, but found that breathing, in or out, was out of the question. I didn't even have the reserve left to roll my eyes. I could feel myself to be an ashen white and an early sweat breaking out on the brow.

Well all this seemed to me to take about a year, but in fact I'm a fast, intelligent thinker and a man of action to boot, and shortly before I died of pain, I regrabbed the wooden handle to thrust it into the take off position once more and thus release the two and a half pounds of mincemeat which used to be the back of my legs. However, the best laid plans etc., and either my agony was so marked or my arms so strong I don't know, but the plain fact is that I simply snapped the handle off, without, I very much regret to say, having thrown it into the desired gear first.

Reservations

At this point my elderly couple – who had been simpering fondly at my erstwhile adulations, and continued to do so after the rat trap closed on me, unaware that all was not well – suddenly realised that the doctor was smashing their new furniture, and began to express reservations.

I began to envy the victims of the Inquisition because at least they had the comfort of knowing that they were documented as condemned and that at the conclusion of a statutory amount of suffering they would be dispatched, whereas here I was with this jibbering pair of nitwits bleating about spoiling their lousy chair, unable or unwilling to comprehend that we were going to spend the rest of our lives disagreeing in each other's company unless they did something to relax their aggressive furniture.

Well I won't bore you with the details. It took time and tediously shouted explanations and directions and wrestling with the bloody thing, while the old dame twittered and made tea, and at last I was free, and they were mollified to see that the damage to my legs at least equated the broken wooden handle, and we parted quits.

Commotion

Mind you, the commotion had penetrated the thin wall to the pensioner unit next door and, when I emerged into the road at last, another elderly couple was standing there hoping for an explanation for the rumpus. I obliged gruffly.

'Their new chair, I had some trouble with it and I got wedged in it.'

'Eh?' said the old guy, cupping his ear.

'I got stuck in the new chair,' I shouted.

His eyes nearly popped out of his head, then, to his ancient spouse, 'Come away and cover your ears, Mabel, he's a naughty rude man.'

One of Those Days

I was watching the French Open (tennis on clay courts for the uninitiated) on the TV the other week, and was constrained to remark to my good woman, sitting next to me, that I thought it was a bit below the belt to have to suffer French advertisements at the same time.

Periodically, throughout the matches, the word EGALITE was flashed on the screen, obviously a sister product to 'Foodalite' – or whatever it is – available over here for slimming. I think they could have left it off the overseas transmission, it's bad enough having to put up with our own adverts.

A quaint habit

And there was another thing I noticed, which I expect escaped those less perspicacious than myself (I'm pretty good on foreign films). This was that whenever one of the players won a game, they flashed his name on the screen – a rather nice, if quaint, habit. But what I noticed so alertly was that an unusual number of the players had the same Christian name, viz Jeu. I had no idea.

Even Edburg – who until then, I was under the impression, was called Stefan, however spelt – was called Jeu. It really was quite a coincidence when you think about it (I mean it's not a common name) for so many at one tennis tournament to share it, even the Russian – perhaps he is a Western Orthodox Christian or something. Well, anyhow, I thought you would like that morsel.

New disease

Then there was the patient of mine who came to see me after that melanoma publicity campaign we had last year, when they told the public what sort of macroscopic features to beware of in skin lesions. 'What's this new disease they're onto us about, Doc? I've never heard of it before. The guy on the radio said we had to look all over our bodies for Asymmetry, but frankly, Doc, I wouldn't know a patch of Asymmetry if I did have one.'

At times I feel as if I'm fighting a lone battle. All around me these irregularities and misunderstandings. I was waiting to pay my bill in one of these huge garages that sell everything from toothbrushes to coal, when my gaze lit on a selection of thermometers on the counter, all of the same make and pattern, labelled 'Made in England', and being promoted for use in the making of home brew. Even casual perusal revealed that in the ambient temperature they were all reading differently, indeed there was a variation of 10.5 degrees between the highest and the lowest. No wonder so many home brews are so frightful ...

Fiendish accuracy

Then we have those fiendishly accurate digital clocks which simply cannot be wrong. We have one by our bedside as part of a radio and alarm clock device, you know the sort I mean, and very useful it is when it knows its place. But when it begins to taunt, as it did one night, I could shoot it between the numerals.

It happened that I couldn't sleep, a rare phenomenon indeed for me, and if there's going to be any doubt, three minutes flat with a medical journal will have me so deeply unconscious that apnoea beings to threaten. But this assumes that I start off with the light on, and on this occasion I had just returned from a night call and I didn't want to disturb the Better Half, so I crept into the sack and lay there, awaiting Morpheus.

The digital alarm radio thing balefully glowed 12.31 a.m. at me. Good oh, I thought, hours and hours to go yet, and I shut my eyes, composed, and waited. After a very considerable time, I turned over to be more comfortable, and in doing so, happened to notice the clock again. To my astonishment it registered 12.32 a.m.

Slow

Reflecting sleepily on how very slow that minute had been I dozed. A lot. On and on. Dozed more. But never quite got off. By Jove, I though I'll have to hurry if I'm not to be yawning all day tomorrow, the night is slipping away. Well, I wonder if there's much more than an hour left before breakfast now, and deliberately looked at the dial. You guessed it. 12.34 a.m.

Eight hours to go before breakfast. So I lay there and recalled to myself my entire life, starting from weaning, as far as I could be sure, and moving in the finest detail through the next fifty years plus a little bit. This took me up to 1.14 a.m., which encouraged me a bit (although I was troubled to notice that it had taken me until 1.12 a.m. to get to the age of twenty-five, and only two minutes for the next twenty-five years, implying that the last quarter century of my life had been mortifyingly uneventful, or my cerebral powers have already so rotted that my lack of recent recall embraces twenty-five years).

Well it certainly was a tiresome night, entirely governed by that evil glowing light which I simply had to look at every few minutes. At 5.45 a.m. my concentration lapsed and I slipped off, just for a second, knowing that I must be up by 7 a.m., and when the second was up, I opened my eyes and glanced at the infernal machine – which to my horror read 8.50 a.m.

A bad time

It was a bad time (forgive the pun) for clocks and the like, because later that day my watch stopped. Not perhaps of itself a unique event, but when I tell you that that was the first time it had stopped since my father gave it to me in 1947, you will appreciate the impact it had on me, not any lessened by another breakdown – my umbrella. By great coincidence the same trusty instrument that I have toted since student days with nary a hitch in its performance, collapsed in a wet, enveloping shroud about my head as several of its ribs gave way later that day.

I'm quite used to my car breaking down, likewise the tele, the lux, the chainsaw, the mower and all the other throwaway, shoddy goods they turn out these days. But when it comes to the fundamentals, made to last a lifetime like Tower Bridge and the Rock of Gibraltar, when all these items belonging to one person pack up, the inescapable conclusion comes in blindingly clearly. And I was not made any happier when, as a sort of finale for the day, I met a chap I hadn't seen in years who greeted me with, 'Well, well, well, and how are things after a decade of retirement?'

To All Intents and Purposes

It's very difficult when you are doing something rather peculiar, to all appearances, in public, but which has perfectly rational explanation.

I have a PO Box (which used to be sited in the post office of yesteryear but is now built into the wall of our local newsagent, so perhaps it should be called a Post Shop Box?) and to empty it I stand on the pavement in the street and shovel the daily offering into a bag. Thankfully the box is at shoulder height, not like some which are so low that their owners have to grovel on their knees to scoop out their bills and junk. Remember its height, because it comes into what I'm about to tell you.

I had been nagging the newsagent for some time to get me a selection of farming magazines which my son overseas wanted me to send to him, and on this particular morning, along with my bills and junk, there were several such agricultural gems, and I was in the process of extracting them when the voice of the newsagent emanated from the box.

'I've got most of what you wanted, Doc.'

'Thank you very much.'

'You can pay me later.'

'I'd rather do it now.'

'I don't know what the price is for two of them yet.'

'Which ones didn't you manage to get?'

'The *Furrow* and, er, I can't remember the other offhand.'

'I think it would be *Manure Monthly*.'

'I'll keep trying.'

'Thanks because he does like *Manure*, he devours it from cover to cover, as it were.'

And so on, really quite simple and much less trouble than going all the way round to the shop door and up to the counter, but you can see, can't you, why old Mrs Wilson, leaning on her stick at the bus stop a few paces away was eyeing me with reservation.

'I saw him with my own eyes. I tell you, Mabel, he was talking to himself. I thought he was going to do something desperate as he said he was going to do it now, but then he went on about manure something awful; I couldn't repeat what he said.'

I never talk to my PO Box now.

Blowing in the wind

And then there was the time that the piece of paper blew away out of my hand, and on that paper was written the name and address of a patient who was acutely and seriously ill and I was just leaving my rooms to visit the patient. Now I know it sounds improbable, and it was, but I assure you most earnestly that such was the case – I had not actually read what was written on the paper, and my nurse, who had taken the message and written it, merely told me it was fairly urgent. We had just been locking up at the end of evening surgery when the call came in, and she was already speeding off down the motorway when the piece of paper blew out of my hand, as I, mind on some imminent maternity, was hurrying to my car.

There was a swirly wind and it swirled my vital message tantalisingly away from me as I tried to put my foot on it. It pirouetted into the air, and danced in the evening sky, just beyond my reach, and then, enough of this frivolity, a strong masterful gust took it up, up and away, straight along the road, as I sprinted up at 35 mph (in those days) after it, and then up into the old silver birch tree outside the church, to lodge in a crevice in the rough bark some thirty feet above my head.

There was nothing for it. Not helped by my overcoat (but I had feared to waste one single second in removing it lest I lost sight of the paper), I climbed the spiked railings of the church boundary. The trunk of the tree had no branches near the ground, but I gained access to the tree by standing on the headstone of the late Joshua Grimble, 1892 to 1922, RIP, and then leaping, Tarzan-like (that is, Tarzan in an overcoat) so that I swung on a lower branch to gain a higher one.

Distracted from below

Then followed a difficult climb, but there was no choice. Nearing the target now, I was distracted suddenly by someone shouting at me from the ground below.

'Are you alright, Doc?'

I recognised one of my more boozy patients, on his way home from the hotel, no doubt. The tone of his voice suggested, through the alcohol, that he was not meaning my physical status so much as querying my motives.

I shouted down my reason for tree climbing.

'You mean that scrap of paper above your head, to the left a bit?' he replied.

'Yes,' I said.

'It's just blown away,' he said.

I looked in time to see it flutter over the wall of a nearby garden, then drop out of sight.

When I had descended and reclimbed back over the spiked railings I hastened to the wall, around to a gateway in it, and into a shrubbery of a private house, whose I knew not, to search. A lady called from a window in the house.

'What do you think you are doing?'

'Looking for some paper.' I was breathless, and anyhow … there was a pause. I suddenly realised the hideousness of what I had said and how it seemed.

'Go away you horrid man or I'll call the police. There are conveniences down the road by the station.'

Greeks Bearing Gifts?

The Hippocratic Oath ensures that we do it all for altruistic motives, but it is economically convenient to be paid as well.

It is even nicer to receive gifts, all the more so if they are surprises, and even more so because at the time of writing they remain free of tax, although I must admit that I have only once in thirty years received any bequest which merited the attention of my accountant, who laughed. The majority have been trivial in the extreme. For example there was the old soul whom I had to visit thrice weekly to give injections, and on each occasion she used to insist that I accept what was, and possibly still is, known as a blackball, an odious boiled sweet with a liquorice flavour. On each occasion I palmed the offending confection but took care to speak lopsidedly so that she thought it was in my cheek, and once outside the house, I cast the horrible thing over the wall into some bushes. I did this for several years, three blackballs a week until they invented tablets better than the injections. The wall was over eight feet high, and what must have been a mighty pyramid of blackballs never actually appeared in view from our side, but I like to think of the archaeologists some hundreds of years hence and wonder what they will decide about this amazingly concentrated deposit of liquorice in just one spot in South Island, New Zealand.

And then there were the turnips – or rather red swedes. There are lots of farms around here and their owners get ill like anyone else. In this case it was a farmer's wife, who, after a very long illness, passed to that big paddock in the sky, whence she beamed down all the right weather to make turnips – or red swedes – grow very well, and her husband's crop prospered to the extent that, when he gathered it in, it constituted a pile of roots something the shape and size of the Albert Hall. It was about then that he took me aside and with moist eyes and much pumping of the hand told me how much he had appreciated my care of his late wife, and how he wanted me to have a present as well as the cheque for my account. And still the penny hadn't dropped for me. He led me out to the yard, to the turnip (or red swede) Albert Hall. Good Lord, I thought, he's going to give me 8,000 tons of turnips. Well he wasn't. 'There you are, Doc,' he said, 'have one. Go on, pick any one you'd like.'

I never learn. There was the late Mrs Finden-Bottingley – in fact there still is the Late Mrs Finden-Bottingley. Read on. The patient, whose full name was Emily Transom Josephine Finden-Bottingley was another who required many months, indeed years, of medical care, all as house visits since she was confined to bed for most of that time until her demise. After that I didn't give her a lot of thought until one day her daughter rang me up, thanking me for the care of

Mama, and then adding that she was now in a position to carry out one of her late mother's last wishes and present to me something which her mother wanted me to have, something which I had often admired and which now would be mine, my very own, to keep. She preferred not to tell me what it was until I could go round to the house and be presented with it. I did have a fairly roomy car, did I?

Yes, indeed I did have; whatever had I admired that big? A 4' by 3' Constable? A rosewood bureau? A pair of Chippendales, perhaps. Not jewellery, one didn't need a big car to remove jewellery unless it was earrings, bracelets and necklaces, diamonds by the sackful; nor silver cigarette boxes. Possible a Persian carpet? I may as well admit I drove round there pretty nippily, scorning the use of all four wheels on the corners, and took the car all the way up the drive to the house since I didn't want the daughter to get a hernia helping me to carry out what must by now be the refectory table, or more likely, the Welsh dresser. I burst in the door, and arrowed up to the erstwhile bedroom I knew so well. The daughter showed me in. 'There!' she said with obvious pleasure and magnanimity.

I looked. Then I looked harder. Then some more. 'Um,' I said. Then, 'Where?'

'There,' she said again, rather in the tone of one having to actually delineate a gorilla in a bathtub for the observer. 'The Spaturans Hemiflorate Clarksii,' she explained.

'Eh?' I replied, wondering if I was beginning to get meningitis, and was really home in bed with cold compresses on my head.

'The potted plant,' she said, unmistakably exasperated by now, speaking as if I had to lip read.

I'm sure you've done it. You visit these dear old

crones so often, and after a while there really isn't a lot of doctoring to perform, and the weather palls as the only topic of conversation, and you shift from one foot to the other, flick imaginary specks of dust off your suit, take your glasses off, then slowly put them on again, and admire things in the room ... but dear Lord, how did I ever come to be so outright negligent as to admire that frightful cruddy old potted half-dead plastic-looking eyesore. Choked with emotion (but not the sort that Emily Transom's daughter thought that she was witnessing), I lugged the gruesome vegetable home, and we left it in the garage, hoping that it would do the decent thing and follow its mistress upstairs. But it didn't; it flourished. We left it out 'by mistake' in the frost, but it did even better. We moved it too close to the garden burner, and it thrived. I couldn't remember its name so we called it The Late Mrs Finden-Bottingley, not out of any lack of respect for the lady, but we all knew what it was we were talking about then. We pruned it severely, we cut it back with axes, but everything pleased it and it threatened to take over the whole place, so one day I took it to the tip and cast it from me. It rooted swiftly and grew and grew, and the last I heard was that the council was going to try and destroy it with explosives. To date, the Late Mrs Finden-Bottingley is alive and well. The mayor and the clerk-of-works have resigned; some trouble at the tip, I'm told, of which I know nothing.

Initially

When I was a house surgeon, I recall a local general practitioner coming to the ward to visit one of his patients. Later, he took me to one side and asked, 'What is this drug, digoxin, and what does it do?'

Now I'm not that old, and I still think he should have known better than that, but, over time, I have acquired a quiet understanding of his problem. Some five years ago, I did a count at the medical school library, and found that there were some forty-seven medical journals published each week to skim through, if one wished to really keep up with the trends. In general practice alone there were, I think, about 3.7 per week. Well, that is fair enough, there is a lot to say, and many people saying it, not like in the days when Freud was able to command an almost empty field.

Now, however, we have the Initials Syndrome, or IS. This is an insidious epidemic which has spread from Europe (the Americans are quite different – they prefer explicit verbosity, e.g. 'two times' for twice, and 'floor coverings' for mats, perhaps TT and FC respectively in the UK). Thus, you can go into the corner shop in Bristol or Birmingham and ask the foreigner behind the counter, 'F U N E X?', and he may reply, 'S V F X'. Translated, 'Have you any eggs?', 'Yes, we have eggs'.

This curious business has found a wealth of application in medicine. We are all familiar with ECG and CXR, UTI, MSU, IDK, and IHD; I'm working on CEA and ERCP, but STD is not all to do with toll calls. The funny thing is, they usually turn out to be short for the American verbosity; 'coronary', though loose, used to serve well for MI; I knew what it was at once without having to think. Now I have to translate in my mind because (and this is what irritates) everyone in one speciality knows what their set of idiotic initials stand for, but everyone else doesn't. One feels stupid having to ask, to which, of course, one's colleague may look supercilious and, if he doesn't know either, he buffles it, just like when you ask an aficionado what Picasso is all about; or he roars with Blenheimer breath and says, 'Beats me, old chap, left all that behind a long time ago.' Reference books don't have indexes of initials so you can't look them up unless you know what they stand for. Catch 22.

Creatures of Habit

If the same person uses the same knife, spoon and fork for every meal for many years, those same utensils will become ground down into a shape uniquely characteristic of that person, a fact that might, but has not, as far as I am aware, been used by detectives for solving crimes.

Perhaps there are not that many gastronomic crimes around, I don't know. However, the amazing fact remains, just as I believe that it is a scientific fact that you always put one sock or one shoe on before the other. Um, yes, well, of course you do, but what I mean is you always put the same one on first; on the same leg. I think I've made the point. Forget it.

I return to ground-down cutlery, and I have a patient, an ancient widower, who had developed such methodical ways in his decades of solo housekeeping that, as soon as he finishes a meal, he washes and dries the plate and knife, fork and spoon and replaces all four items on the table ready for the next repast. Thus for thirty years none of the other eating irons in the cupboard have been used, and the result is that he is using three handles from which protrude what can just be recognised as the asymmetrically worn away remnants of a knife, fork and spoon. I hope he leaves them to me in his will, and then I will try and sell them to the British Museum as Bronze Age relics.

Protocols

The point of all I'm saying, as the better educated amongst my readers will have divined (unlike the MP, a current Cabinet Minister, no less, who wrote to me lately including the phrase "with the time which has past"), is that we chaps are pretty good at 'batching', given time to settle in and evolve a bit of routine, because it is, like so many things, a matter of method and planning, as I think Hercule Poirot was wont to say. My better half is seldom ill or away from home for long, touch wood, but over the years she has been both, occasionally, and I have formulated a few protocols from my experience which might be of value to you.

One of these is never to be overawed by 'the washing'. When my great-great-great-great-grandmother used to beat the smocks and hose on rocks in the stream, and then have to dry them in a hurry lest a sabre-toothed tiger nabbed her on leaving the cave, yes, then it was quite a hassle. These days admittedly you have to walk all the way to the washing machine because they haven't got an infrared thing to switch it on remotely with, but after that it's all downhill. You p-r-e-s-s a b-u-t-t-o-n. Later in the day you iron the clothes. Not too bad, was it?

Ironing is quite fun. You crush everything out flat … or in whatever shape you fancy, you just press on – ha ha! I have to confess that I have never quite mastered the shirt, a tricky garment because people can see it and wonder why you have one half of the collar twice as big as the other, and a prominent fold or corner diagonally across your left chest.

And for a long time sheets had me beaten. Try as I may, I could not find a larger size of ironing board anywhere in the house or in shops, but, never at a loss, I solved the problem neatly by shifting the dining room table against the wall, piling the chairs up in the hall, putting the iron on a long extension cord, and doing the sheets on the dining room floor. You have to be careful though to make sure where you start and finish because it is all too easy to end up on the other side of the room, and the sheet – rather like sitting on the branch you are sawing off – and find you have to make a standing leap of Olympian standard to get back to base, as it were. I've learned by experience but I thought I'd save you the trouble.

In a nutshell

That's it, really. Housekeeping in a nutshell. Can't think of anything I've missed. Well, luxing, of course. It's a bit like the washing, only less. When you see the inadvertent footmark on the pile carpet, you lux it off. Rest of the day's your own.

I should add that you have to eat, although it scarcely ranks as work. You just eat whatever you like, whenever you like, and as much of it as you like. I cannot cook, which limits my menu slightly. I can boil things, but I cannot in all honesty count that as cordon bleu. I have three items I boil, and these are mashed potato, leeks and smoked fish, and I repeat these dishes so often that the rather pungent odour from the leeks and smoked fish gets kind of stuck in the house; I become used to it because I am in the house, but visitors have been known to be paralysed at the front door, their friends dragging them away for resuscitation despite my entreaties that all is well and the drains fluent.

I am not a vegetarian, so, I hear you ask, where does the protein come in? In a word – tins. Lambs' tongues, half a tin per meal, average one tin per day i.e. fourteen per fortnight or thirty per month, so my order to the grocer reads: "Rx. Tongues, lambs, tins of, Mitte 30, Sig half-tin b.d., Ext Supply 3/12."

Last time I was batching for longer than usual because the dear O.L. had the vile shingles, and our local grocer had to send to his wholesaler for another truckload of tongues, which reminds me of very dim dark ages of yore when I shared digs in London with another medical student. In those days they hadn't invented lambs' tongues, but the Irish, God bless them, had invented sheeps' hearts (tinned, of course, or they would have been no use to us). A seedy shop off Tottenham Court Road must have bought a cheap lot, a crate or three, from the Emerald Isle. Anyhow, they had several thousand tins of heart displayed on a top shelf. It took Dave and I eighteen months to eat our way through the entire importation, but we managed it in the end, and after that there was no alternative but to qualify and go and be a hospital-fed house surgeon.

Sorely missed

And I would be guilty of omission if I failed to tell you of how sorely I missed the lady wife the last time she was away and I was running the household in my impeccable way. One night I was very tired and went to bed early, and slept the sleep of the innocent. I awoke as it was getting light, refreshed and ready to go, eager for my chores of washing, luxing, tin opening, etc. When I'm on my own, I turn off my wife's luminous alarm machine because I dislike it talking inanities to me at dawn, and my watch is not luminous, but, as I said, it was getting light and I padded downstairs in my dressing gown, let the cat in, filled its food bowl, chucked wood on the stove, put on the kettle and sought out an unused tea bag. In passing, my eye took in the luminous clock on the electric range. 1.40 a.m. I snatched back the nearest curtains. Brilliant moonlight flooded the garden. I turned the kettle off, closed the damper on the stove, ejected the still chewing and totally mystified cat, ascended the stairs, removed the dressing gown, and lay in bed for a further six hours, feeling the slightest teeny bit foolish.

Shipwreck

I'm not a camping man, never was. Having spent a life's earnings on a comfortable house with running water, flush toilets, furniture, refrigerator and bath, I like to use them. I see no point in shivering in a tent, shaving in a stream and sitting over a hole. For me, the gleaming porcelain, a glass of whisky, an upholstered leather chair, and sleeping between clean sheets on a mattress on a bed.

I tried camping once, deliberately, and it was awful. It was forced on me a second time, and it was worse, but we carried it off in style.

The setting was the Nelson coastline which we (self and two sons aged ten and twelve) were skirting in a motorboat, hired to take us down the bays to friends in their 'crib', a lavishly furnished house with all mod cons which thoroughly merited my approbation. A leg of ham and a one gallon flask of wine was all our luggage, a symbolic gift to our hostess, knowing that all else would be provided at our destination. Younger son had a gigantic hunting knife tucked into his sock simply because it was a Christmas present from which he would not be parted.

These then were the actors and props when the weather blew up nasty. I was violently seasick, and our boatman elected to land us rather than drown us. There was, he said, a hut on a walking track where we could stay the night and he would pick us up again in the morning when the weather had improved. I nodded mutely, too green and bilious to care, and shortly after we were trudging up the beach like three Robinson Crusoes, (or one R Crusoe and two Men Friday), to find a big wooden hut in the forest, nearly full of jolly trampers, all vigorous young people from Canada, Germany, America, France, Israel and Switzerland. All equipped with sleeping bags, toilet paper, cups, cutlery, tea, milk, sugar, and delicious smelling rice risottos and things which they cooked and ate and then sat around the fire, yarning.

We had none of these; my nausea had worn off and the boys were ravenous ... Yes, well, there was nothing for it, was there? The three of us sat on the bench near the fire and solemnly passed around the leg of ham, the hunting knife, and the flagon of wine. Insouciance, I think, is the word. Hack a hunk off, chew it, wash it down with a swig of Chardonnay, pass it on to the next. The yarning trampers grew silent. We ate on, stolidly. We had the same for pudding. 'Mein Gott,' exclaimed our audience, then whispered, 'Dose are Herr Kiwis.'

Simon, the last to finish, wiped the hunting knife blade on his thigh for want of anything else, and replaced it in his sock. 'Sacre Bleu', in awe, from the overseas contingent. Then trips to the loo, tearing generous handfuls of foliage from the bush on the way, in lieu of the usual roll. 'Holy Cow,' said a Yank. The reverence was unmistakable.

'Bed' that night was an ordeal. We lay on a big wooden shelf, the three of us, side by side, dressed as we were, and stared at the ceiling. It was hot, and we ran with sweat, but dared not expose more flesh than was essential because of golf ball sized sand flies. Someone shone a torch on us once or twice. 'Oi vai,' it said.

After eight hours we stood up, sat on the bench, and repeated our Henry VIII ritual with the ham, wine and knife, for breakfast. Our continental colleagues completely dispensed with eating their own for the privilege of watching us training to be All Blacks. A Swiss girl nervously approached.

'M'sieur, ees zees all you 'ave?'

'Yup.'

'Jeeze,' said the Yank.

'Are you on holiday or probation?' asked a Canadian.

'Holiday.' (Notice again the insouciance.)

'For FUN?'

'Yup.'

'Mon Dieu.'

Simon did his act, re-socking the knife.

'Donner und Blitzen, no vonder dey von de var.'

We rose, and their ranks parted courteously to let us through.

We walked with careful dignity down the beach. The boat approached, we got in and puttered away. A respectful line of them stood at the water's edge. Above the hum of the motor and the lap of the waves, we heard a communal sigh:

'Jeeeeeeeeeze.'

The Kumara

(To save the ignorami thrashing a sleepless pillow, a kumara is a sweet potato in New Zealand, and is pronounced 'Koomerer'. Read on.)

All my tales are based on fact; some are gospel truth. This one is. Not even the names are changed because, in a tiny way, I like to believe that it could be a sort of epitaph to those involved: two patients with whom I have laughed and joked with so much enjoyment over the last thirty-one years.

I write this with the certain knowledge that both are looking down from above and laughing yet again at something that perhaps only the three of us could have achieved, albeit unintentionally.

Ngaire and Len lived next door to each other. Each had lost their spouse some years ago and both were middle-aged invalids themselves, Ngaire from heart disease and Len with emphysema. Many times one had cut the other's hedge or lawn while the other was in hospital; each knew the secret hiding place for the front door key of the other. They ferried each other to my rooms, when fit enough, or collected each other's prescriptions from the chemist when I had visited. Neither had breath to spare, but we often told stories and cracked silly jokes until all three of us were gasping for air.

Natural clown

Ngaire, in particular, was one of this world's natural clowns and on one occasion had an entire supermarket in hysterics when her salad dressing container burst over everything else, including the electronic eye thing at the checkout counter.

And so it was that, on one of Len's last admissions to hospital, she went to visit him in the ward. On the way, she called at the greengrocer's, amongst other things buying him a succulent bunch of grapes, and herself some vegetables for the evening meal. However, on arrival at the ward, Len was not conscious, and, after waiting by the bedside for a bit, she placed the brown paper bag containing the grapes on his bedside locker, and tiptoed away. Later in the day, she went to make tea, and on opening the brown paper bag, which she knew contained kumaras, was horrified to perceive a luscious bunch of grapes.

At about the same time, Len was coming around a bit and when the nurse pointed out to him that a visitor had left him a wee present, he opened the brown paper bag and drew out a couple of kumaras, one still with an abundance of earth on it.

'Oh my,' said the nurse, to which Len replied with less politeness.

Then he pulled his oxygen mask to one side. 'Was my visitor female?'

'Yes.'

'Was she short, with curly hair?'

'Yes'

'And with a loopy smile on her face?'

'Well, you are quite ill and she didn't smile all that much, but, yes, she did smile easily.'

'I know, I know. She's iller than I am. Wait till I get home.'

'Now, now, just take deep breaths on the mask; it'll make you feel better.'

'Nothing will make me feel better until I've had a word with Ngaire.'

Well of course we all laughed about that one for a long time after, but sad to relate Len succumbed one day before Ngaire was able to turn up with a bunch of grapes or even a good-wish card.

Then we move on about three months to 7.30 a.m. one day when my phone rang and a croaking voice in my ear announced herself as: 'This is Ngaire, I'm bleeding terribly, this is awful, I've never had this before, come at once …' Then the phone became ominously silent and it sounded as if my caller had fallen over. There was a bump sound, anyhow.

Not that rare

Now because you are reading this story about Ngaire of kumara fame, it is easy for you to know at once that it was she, but at the time I was just shaving my face and not a single Ngaire was crossing my mind. Indeed, if my memory serves, I was indulging in my continuous and continual reverie about what I would do if I won Lotto.

I have no way of knowing with how many Ngaires you are acquainted, either through business or pleasure, but it is not that rare a name, and straight off I was able to think of six, one of whom was so ill that her voice was not readily identifiable. I suppose it would have been possible to try phoning all six, and with a bit of luck the one who failed to reply would be the one lying on the floor by her phone.

But even to the dullest dreamer about Lotto it was clear that time was of the essence, and I hastily pulled on a minimum of clothing, during the course of which I (fortunately, as it turned out) changed my first choice Ngaire from a lady I'd seen recently with asthma to another with the same to, thirdly, Ngaire of the kumara. I'm not sure why, there must have been something in her voice after all.

I asked my wife to call the ambulance and vector it after me towards that Ngaire, and as I drove across town to her address I wondered what I would say to the ambulance men if we found the good lady at the breakfast cornflakes and *Otago Daily Times* astonished by our heroic arrival. 'Hello, Ngaire, how nice to see you. Right, chaps, back in the van, follow me.'

And what indeed if the second or, heaven forbid, even the third Ngaire were the wrong ones? And even as I drove, I was able to call to mind a seventh, eighth and ninth Ngaire. The world was loaded with them. Why couldn't very urgently ill people be called Eubula de Mathingholde for quick and easy identification?

Severe bleed

Well it was the right one in the event, the kumara one, and guess what, she had a Mallory-Weiss tear from laughing so much about something that it made her ill … literally. She certainly had a very severe bleed and in no time at all was in hospital with all the right things being done, sitting up and giving cheek, and it was a couple of days later when a childish prank occurred to me. I like to visit my customers in hospital when possible, and I anticipated how Ngaire would laugh when I told her about my fears of dragging the ambulance around all the Ngaires in the city until we struck one ill enough to take to hospital. On the way to the hospital, I called in at a greengrocer's and purchased a kumara in a brown paper bag.

Once in the ward there was no sign of my patient, whereupon the sister broke the news that, yes, she had responded well to treatment for the haemorrhage, but during the night had had a heart attack and was now in the Intensive Care ward.

It was very quiet there; Ngaire was unconscious, surrounded by, and attached to, all the sophisticated modern day equipment, drips, tubes, monitors, wires, and attended by two doctors and three nurses, all specialists in their field, all in gowns and masks.

The senior doctor knew me at once, welcoming me cordially by my Christian name. But then his tone became grey.

'We've given it our best, old man, our very best.'

The superlative could only mean one thing.

'No tricks up the sleeve?' I said.

Softly, 'No.'

'Well,' I said (always a good start when you don't know what to say). 'Well thank you anyhow'; and, lamely, 'You never know.'

I never knew before how much some patients meant to me.

'Yes,' he said.

'So I'll be off now; only in your way here.'

Suddenly I remembered I was holding a brown paper bag. On impulse I placed it on the bedside table, amongst all the clever equipment.

'Just in case she does wake up,' I said.
Silence.
They all looked at me again, over their masks.
'It's a kumara,' I said.
Five pairs of eyes blinked. No one spoke.
I turned and hurried away.

Conclusion

In 2005 I received a letter from the President of the Royal College of General Practitioners, congratulating me on achieving, in my retirement, Life Membership of the College, and advising that henceforth I would therefore not be required to pay any more annual subscriptions. Included with his letter was a plastic membership card.

I replied as follows:

'Dear Dr Neighbour,

Thank you for your kind letter regarding my imminent accession to Life Membership of the College.

However, I am dismayed by the card which reads "Life Member. Expiry date 31st March 2006".

This lugubrious prognosis fills me with awe at its precision; clearly huge strides have been made in this field since I retired, but I had hoped for a bit longer, although I admit my three score and ten is already up. I had particularly wanted to visit my sister in Devon in September.

Could my case not be reviewed, and, in the event of my surviving beyond 31.3.06, perhaps my executors could pencil in when the card becomes invalid? The College could then ink it in to preserve the accuracy of its records, and I could visit my sister.

I am confident that you will appreciate my concern. Yours etc.'

The President replied in good heart but made no promises.

It's snowing gently and when it does I always feel a great peace. Something like in autumn, when the russet leaves fall with a clump every now and then. There's a tranquillity about it, nature taking no notice of these pygmy men at the stock exchange, the farm, the wharf, the railway station. The snow flakes large and, like butterflies, sprinkle down, one or two cover a penny, but now, in their millions, they mutely coat the landscape in white. There's no wind, they say it is from Siberia, but nothing stirs. The temperature is O degrees, neither more nor less. Gently snowing, it's like making the bed after a hectic night of love-making, a summer of high endeavour, and warm reward. Now it's tidied up, under a mantle of peace and rest. It's how we shall all be, one day.

NEVER MIND.